THE PHANTOM 'RICKSHAW
AND OTHER MYSTERIES

The Works of

Rudyard Kipling

The Phantom 'Rickshaw

Volume VIII

THE WORLD SYNDICATE PUBLISHING CO.
CLEVELAND, O.   NEW YORK, N. Y.

Printed in the United States of America

CONTENTS

PREFACE

THIS is not exactly a book of downright ghost-stories as the cover makes belief. It is rather a collection of facts that never quite explained themselves. All that the collector is certain of is, that one man insisted upon dying because he believed himself to be haunted; another man either made up a wonderful lie and stuck to it, or visited a very strange place; while the third man was indubitably crucified by some person or persons unknown, and gave an extraordinary account of himself.

The peculiarity of ghost-stories is that they are never told first-hand. I have managed, with infinite trouble, to secure one exception to this rule. It is not a very good specimen, but you can credit it from beginning to end. The other three stories you must take on trust; as I did.

RUDYARD KIPLING.

THE PHANTOM 'RICKSHAW

THE PHANTOM 'RICKSHAW

May no ill dreams disturb my rest,
Nor Powers of Darkness me molest.
                    —*Evening Hymn.*

ONE of the few advantages that India has over England is a great Knowability. After five years' service a man is directly or indirectly acquainted with the two or three hundred Civilians in his Province, all the Messes of ten or twelve Regiments and Batteries, and some fifteen hundred other people of the non-official caste. In ten years his knowledge should be doubled, and at the end of twenty he knows, or knows something about, every Englishman in the Empire, and may travel anywhere and everywhere without paying hotel-bills.

Globe-trotters who expect entertainment as a right, have, even within my memory, blunted this open-heartedness, but none the less to-day, if you belong to the Inner Circle and are neither a Bear nor a Black Sheep, all houses are open to you, and our small world is very, very kind and helpful.

Rickett of Kamartha stayed with Polder of

Kumaon some fifteen years ago. He meant to stay two nights, but was knocked down by rheumatic fever, and for six weeks disorganized Polder's establishment, stopped Polder's work, and nearly died in Polder's bedroom. Polder behaves as though he had been placed under eternal obligation by Rickett, and yearly sends the little Ricketts a box of presents and toys. It is the same everywhere. The men who do not take the trouble to conceal from you their opinion that you are an incompetent ass, and the women who blacken your character and misunderstand your wife's amusements, will work themselves to the bone in your behalf if you fall sick or into serious trouble.

Heatherlegh, the Doctor, kept, in addition to his regular practice, a hospital on his private account —an arrangement of loose boxes for Incurables, his friend called it—but it was really a sort of fitting-up shed for craft that had been damaged by stress of weather. The weather in India is often sultry, and since the tale of bricks is always a fixed quantity, and the only liberty allowed is permission to work overtime and get no thanks, men occasionally break down and become as mixed as the metaphors in this sentence.

Heatherlegh is the dearest doctor that ever was, and his invariable prescription to all his patients is, "lie low, go slow, and keep cool."

He says that more men are killed by overwork than the importance of this world justifies. He maintains that overwork slew Pansay, who died under his hands about three years ago. He has, of course, the right to speak authoritatively, and he laughs at my theory that there was a crack in Pansay's head and a little bit of the Dark World came through and pressed him to death. "Pansay went off the handle," says Heatherlegh, "after the stimulus of long leave at Home. He may or he may not have behaved like a blackguard to Mrs. Keith-Wessington. My notion is that the work of the Katabundi Settlement ran him off his legs, and that he took to brooding and making much of an ordinary P. & O. flirtation. He certainly was engaged to Miss Mannering, and she certainly broke off the engagement. Then he took a feverish chill and all that nonsense about ghosts developed. Overwork started his illness, kept it alight, and killed him, poor devil. Write him off to the System—one man to take the work of two and a half men."

I do not believe this. I used to sit up with Pansay sometimes when Heatherlegh was called out to patients, and I happened to be within claim. The man would make me most unhappy by describing in a low, even voice, the procession that was always passing at the bottom of his bed. He had a sick man's command of lan-

guage. When he recovered I suggested that he
should write out the whole affair from beginning
to end, knowing that ink might assist him to
ease his mind. When little boys have learned a
new bad word they are never happy till they
have chalked it up on a door. And this also is
Literature.

He was in a high fever while he was writing,
and the blood-and-thunder Magazine diction he
adopted did not calm him. Two months afterward he was reported fit for duty, but, in spite
of the fact that he was urgently needed to help
an undermanned Commission stagger through a
deficit, he preferred to die; vowing at the last
that he was hag-ridden. I got his manuscript
before he died, and this is his version of the
affair, dated 1885:

My doctor tells me that I need rest and change
of air. It is not improbable that I shall get both
ere long—rest that neither the red-coated mes-
senger nor the midday gun can break, and
change of air far beyond that which any home-
ward-bound steamer can give me. In the meantime I am resolved to stay where I am; and, in
flat defiance of my doctor's orders, to take all the
world into my confidence. You shall learn for
yourselves the precise nature of my malady; and
shall, too, judge for yourselves whether any man

born of woman on this weary earth was ever
so tormented as I.

Speaking now as a condemned criminal might
speak ere the drop-bolts are drawn, my story,
wild and hideously improbable as it may appear,
demands at least attention. That it will ever
receive credence I utterly disbelieve. Two
months ago I should have scouted as mad or
drunk the man who had dared tell me the like
Two months ago I was the happiest man in
India. To-day, from Peshawur to the sea, there
is no one more wretched. My doctor and I are
the only two who know this. His explanation
is, that my brain, digestion, and eyesight are all
slightly affected; giving rise to my frequent and
persistent "delusions." Delusions, indeed! I
call him a fool; but he attends me still with the
same unwearied smile, the same bland professional manner, the same neatly trimmed red
whiskers, till I begin to suspect that I am an ungrateful, evil-tempered invalid. But you shall
judge for yourselves.

Three years ago it was my fortune—my great
misfortune—to sail from Gravesend to Bombay,
on return from long leave, with one Agnes
Keith-Wessington, wife of an officer on the
Bombay side. It does not in the least concern
you to know what manner of woman she was.
Be content with the knowledge that, ere the

voyage had ended, both she and I were desperately and unreasoningly in love with one another.
Heaven knows that I can make the admission
now without one particle of vanity. In matters
of this sort there is always one who gives and
another who accepts. From the first day of our
ill-omened attachment, I was conscious that
Agnes's passion was a stronger, a more dominant, and—if I may use the expression—a
purer sentiment than mine. Whether she recognized the fact then, I do not know. Afterward
it was bitterly plain to both of us.

Arrived at Bombay in the spring of the year,
we went our respective ways, to meet no more
for the next three or four months, when my leave
and her love took us both to Simla. There we
spent the season together; and there my fire of
straw burned itself out to a pitiful end with
the closing year. I attempt no excuse. I make
no apology. Mrs. Wessington had given up
much for my sake, and was prepared to give up
all. From my own lips, in August, 1882, she
learned that I was sick of her presence, tired of
her company, and weary of the sound of her
voice. Ninety-nine women out of a hundred
would have wearied of me as I wearied of them;
seventy-five of that number would have promptly
avenged themselves by active and obtrusive flirtation with other men. Mrs. Wessington was the

hundredth. On her neither my openly expressed aversion nor the cutting brutalities with which I garnished our interviews had the least effect.

"Jack, darling!" was her one eternal cuckoo cry: "I'm sure it's all a mistake—a hideous mistake; and we'll be good friends again some day. *Please* forgive me, Jack, dear."

I was the offender, and I knew it. That knowledge transformed my pity into passive endurance, and, eventually, into blind hate—the same instinct, I suppose, which prompts a man to savagely stamp on the spider he has but half killed. And with this hate in my bosom the season of 1882 came to an end.

Next year we met again at Simla—she with her monotonous face and timid attempts at reconciliation, and I with loathing of her in every fibre of my frame. Several times I could not avoid meeting her alone; and on each occasion her words were identically the same. Still the unreasoning wail that it was all a "mistake"; and still the hope of eventually "making friends." I might have seen had I cared to look, that that hope only was keeping her alive. She grew more wan and thin month by month. You will agree with me, at least, that such conduct would have driven any one to despair. It was uncalled for; childish; unwomanly. I maintain that she was much to blame. And again, sometimes, in

the black, fever-stricken night-watches, I have
begun to think that I might have been a little
kinder to her. But that really *is* a "delusion."
I could not have continued pretending to love her
when I didn't; could I? It would have been unfair to us both.

Last year we met again—on the same terms as
before. The same weary appeals, and the same
curt answers from my lips. At least I would
make her see how wholly wrong and hopeless
were her attempts at resuming the old relationship. As the season wore on, we fell apart—
that is to say, she found it difficult to meet me,
for I had other and more absorbing interests to
attend to. When I think it over quietly in my
sick-room, the season of 1884 seems a confused
nightmare wherein light and shade were fan-
tastically intermingled—my courtship of little
Kitty Mannering; my hopes, doubts, and fears;
our long rides together; my trembling avowal of
attachment; her reply; and now and again a
vision of a white face flitting by in the 'rickshaw
with the black and white liveries I once watched
for so earnestly; the wave of Mrs. Wessington's
gloved hand; and, when she met me alone,
which was but seldom, the irksome monotony of
her appeal. I loved Kitty Mannering; honestly,
heartily loved her, and with my love for her grew
my hatred for Agnes. In August Kitty and I

were engaged. The next day I met those accursed "magpie" *jhampanies* at the back of
Jakko, and, moved by some passing sentiment of
pity, stopped to tell Mrs. Wessington everything.
She knew it already.

"So I hear you're engaged, Jack dear." Then,
without a moment's pause:—"I'm sure it's all a
mistake—a hideous mistake. We shall be as
good friends some day, Jack, as we ever were."

My answer might have made even a man wince.
It cut the dying woman before me like the blow
of a whip. "Please forgive me, Jack; I didn't
mean to make you angry; but it's true, it's true!"

And Mrs. Wessington broke down completely.
I turned away and left her to finish her journey
in peace, feeling, but only for a moment or two,
that I had been an unutterably mean hound. I
looked back, and saw that she had turned her
'rickshaw with the idea, I suppose, of overtaking
me.

The scene and its surroundings were photo-
graphed on my memory. The rain-swept sky
(we were at the end of the wet weather), the
sodden, dingy pines, the muddy road, and the
black powder-riven cliffs formed a gloomy back-
ground against which the black and white liveries
of the *jhampanies*, the yellow-paneled 'rickshaw
and Mrs. Wessington's down-bowed golden head
stood out clearly. She was holding her handker-

chief in her left hand and was leaning back exhausted against the 'rickshaw cushions. I turned my horse up a bypath near the Sanjowlie Reservoir and literally ran away. Once I fancied I heard a faint call of "Jack!" This may have been imagination. I never stopped to verify it. Ten minutes later I came across Kitty on horseback; and, in the delight of a long ride with her, forgot all about the interview.

A week later Mrs. Wessington died, and the inexpressible burden of her existence was removed from my life. I went Plainsward perfectly happy. Before three months were over I had forgotten all about her, except that at times the discovery of some of her old letters reminded me unpleasantly of our bygone relationship. By January I had disinterred what was left of our correspondence from among my scattered belongings and had burned it. At the beginning of April of this year, 1885, I was at Simla—semi-deserted Simla—once more, and was deep in lover's talks and walks with Kitty. It was decided that we should be married at the end of June. You will understand, therefore, that, loving Kitty as I did, I am not saying too much when I pronounce myself to have been, at that time, the happiest man in India.

Fourteen delightful days passed almost before I noticed their flight. Then, aroused to the sense of what was proper among mortals circumstanced as we were, I pointed out to Kitty that an engagement ring was the outward and visible sign of her dignity as an engaged girl; and that she must forthwith come to Hamilton's to be measured for one. Up to that moment, I give you my word, we had completely forgotten so trivial a matter. To Hamilton's we accordingly went on the 15th of April, 1885. Remember that—whatever my doctor may say to the contrary—I was then in perfect health, enjoying a well-balanced mind and an *absolutely* tranquil spirit. Kitty and I entered Hamilton's shop together, and there, regardless of the order of affairs, I measured Kitty for the ring in the presence of the amused assistant. The ring was a sapphire with two diamonds. We then rode out down the slope that leads to the Combermere Bridge and Peliti's shop.

While my Waler was cautiously feeling his way over the loose shale, and Kitty was laughing and chattering at my side—while all Simla, that is to say as much of it as had then come from the Plains, was grouped round the Reading-room and Peliti's veranda,—I was aware that some one, apparently at a vast distance, was calling me by my Christian name. It struck me that I had heard the voice before, but when and where I could not at once determine. In the short space it took to cover the road between the path from Hamilton's shop and the first plank of the Combermere Bridge I had thought over half a dozen people who might have committed such a solecism, and had eventually decided that it must have been singing in my ears. Immediately opposite Peliti's shop my eye was arrested by the sight of four *jhampanies* in "magpie" livery, pulling a yellow-paneled, cheap, bazar 'rickshaw. In a moment my mind flew back to the previous season and Mrs. Wessington with a sense of irritation and disgust. Was it not enough that the woman was dead and done with, without her black and white servitors reappearing to spoil the day's happiness? Whoever employed them now I thought I would call upon, and ask as a personal favor to change her *jhampanies*' livery. I would hire the men myself, and, if necessary, buy their coats from off their backs. It is impossible to say here what a flood of undesirable memories their presence evoked.

"Kitty," I cried, "there are poor Mrs. Wessington's *jhampanies* turned up again! I wonder who has them now?"

Kitty had known Mrs. Wessington slightly last season, and had always been interested in the sickly woman.

"What? Where?" she asked. "I can't see them anywhere."

Even as she spoke, her horse, swerving from a laden mule, threw himself directly in front of the advancing 'rickshaw. I had scarcely time to utter a word of warning when, to my unutterable horror, horse and rider passed *through* men and carriage as if they had been thin air.

"What's the matter?" cried Kitty; "what made you call out so foolishly, Jack? If I *am* engaged I don't want all creation to know about it. There was lots of space between the mule and the veranda; and, if you think I can't ride — There!"

Whereupon wilful Kitty set off, her dainty little head in the air, at a hand-gallop in the direction of the Band-stand; fully expecting, as she herself afterward told me, that I should follow her. What was the matter? Nothing indeed. Either that I was mad or drunk, or that Simla was haunted with devils. I reined in my impatient cob, and turned round. The 'rickshaw had turned too, and now stood immediately facing me, near the left railing of the Combermere Bridge.

"Jack! Jack, darling!" (There was no mistake about the words this time: they rang through my brain as if they had been shouted in my ear.) "It's some hideous mistake, I'm sure. *Please* forgive me, Jack, and let's be friends again."

The 'rickshaw-hood had fallen back, and inside, as I hope and pray daily for the death I dread by night, sat Mrs. Keith-Wessington, handkerchief in hand, and golden head bowed on her breast.

How long I stared motionless I do not know. Finally, I was aroused by my syce taking the Waler's bridle and asking whether I was ill. From the horrible to the commonplace is but a step. I tumbled off my horse and dashed, half fainting, into Peliti's for a glass of cherry-brandy. There two or three couples were gathered round the coffee-tables discussing the gossip of the day. Their trivialities were more comforting to me just then than the consolations of religion could have been. I plunged into the midst of the conversation at once; chatted, laughed, and jested with a face (when I caught a glimpse of it in a mirror) as white and drawn as that of a corpse. Three or four men noticed my condition; and, evidently setting it down to the results of over-many pegs, charitably endeavored to draw me apart from the rest of the loungers. But I refused to be led away. I wanted the company of my kind—as a child rushes into the midst of the dinner-party after a fright in the dark. I must have talked for about ten minutes or so, though it seemed an eternity to me, when I heard Kitty's clear voice outside

inquiring for me. In another minute she had
entered the shop, prepared to roundly upbraid
me for failing so signally in my duties. Something in my face stopped her.

"Why, Jack," she cried, "what *have* you
been doing? What *has* happened? Are you
ill?" Thus driven into a direct lie, I said that
the sun had been a little too much for me. It
was close upon five o'clock of a cloudy April
afternoon, and the sun had been hidden all day.
I saw my mistake as soon as the words were out
of my mouth: attempted to recover it; blundered hopelessly and followed Kitty in a regal
rage, out of doors, amid the smiles of my
acquaintances. I made some excuse (I have forgotten what) on the score of my feeling faint;
and cantered away to my hotel, leaving Kitty to
finish the ride by herself.

In my room I sat down and tried calmly to
reason out the matter. Here was I, Theobald
Jack Pansay, a well-educated Bengal Civilian in
the year of grace 1885, presumably sane, certainly healthy, driven in terror from my sweetheart's side by the apparition of a woman who
had been dead and buried eight months ago.
These were facts that I could not blink. Nothing was further from my thought than any
memory of Mrs. Wessington when Kitty and I
left Hamilton's shop. Nothing was more utterly

commonplace than the stretch of wall opposite Peliti's. It was broad daylight. The road was full of people; and yet here, look you, in defiance of every law of probability, in direct outrage of Nature's ordinance, there had appeared to me a face from the grave.

Kitty's Arab had gone *through* the 'rickshaw: so that my first hope that some woman marvelously like Mrs. Wessington had hired the carriage and the coolies with their old livery was lost. Again and again I went round this treadmill of thought; and again and again gave up baffled and in despair. The voice was as inexplicable as the apparition. I had originally some wild notion of confiding it all to Kitty; of begging her to marry me at once; and in her arms defying the ghostly occupant of the 'rickshaw. "After all," I argued, "the presence of the 'rickshaw is in itself enough to prove the existence of a spectral illusion. One may see ghosts of men and women, but surely never of coolies and carriages. The whole thing is absurd. Fancy the ghost of a hillman!"

Next morning I sent a penitent note to Kitty, imploring her to overlook my strange conduct of the previous afternoon. My Divinity was still very wroth, and a personal apology was necessary. I explained, with a fluency born of night-long pondering over a falsehood, that I had been

attacked with a sudden palpitation of the heart—
the result of indigestion. This eminently practical solution had its effect; and Kitty and I rode
out that afternoon with the shadow of my first
lie dividing us.

Nothing would please her save a canter round
Jakko. With my nerves still unstrung from the
previous night I feebly protested against the notion, suggesting Observatory Hill, Jutogh, the
Boileaugunge road—anything rather than the
Jakko round. Kitty was angry and a little hurt:
so I yielded from fear of provoking further mis-
understanding, and we set out together toward
Chota Simla. We walked a greater part of the
way, and, according to our custom, cantered
from a mile or so below the Convent to the
stretch of level road by the Sanjowlie Reservoir.
The wretched horses appeared to fly, and my
heart beat quicker and quicker as we neared the
crest of the ascent. My mind had been full of
Mrs. Wessington all the afternoon; and every
inch of the Jakko road bore witness to our old-
time walks and talks. The bowlders were full
of it; the pines sang it aloud overhead; the
rain-fed torrents giggled and chuckled unseen
over the shameful story; and the wind in my
ears chanted the iniquity aloud.

As a fitting climax, in the middle of the level
men call the Ladies' Mile the Horror was awaiting

me. No other 'rickshaw was in sight—only the four black and white *jhampanies*, the yellow-paneled carriage, and the golden head of the woman within—all apparently just as I had left them eight months and one fortnight ago! For an instant I fancied that Kitty *must* see what I saw—we were so marvelously sympathetic in all things. Her next words undeceived me— "Not a soul in sight! Come along, Jack, and I'll race you to the Reservoir buildings!" Her wiry little Arab was off like a bird, my Waler following close behind, and in this order we dashed under the cliffs. Half a minute brought us within fifty yards of the 'rickshaw. I pulled my Waler and fell back a little. The 'rickshaw was directly in the middle of the road; and once more the Arab passed through it, my horse following. "Jack! Jack dear! *Please* forgive me," rang with a wail in my ears, and, after an interval:— "It's all a mistake, a hideous mistake!"

I spurred my horse like a man possessed. When I turned my head at the Reservoir works, the black and white liveries were still waiting— patiently waiting—under the grey hillside, and the wind brought me a mocking echo of the words I had just heard. Kitty bantered me a good deal on my silence throughout the remainder of the ride. I had been talking up till then wildly and at random. To save my life I could

not speak afterward naturally, and from Sanjowlie to the Church wisely held my tongue.

I was to dine with the Mannerings that night,
and had barely time to canter home to dress.
On the road to Elysium Hill I overheard two men
talking together in the dusk.—"It's a curious
thing," said one, "how completely all trace of it
disappeared. You know my wife was insanely
fond of the woman ('never could see anything in
her myself), and wanted me to pick up her old
'rickshaw and coolies if they were to be got for
love or money. Morbid sort of fancy I call it;
but I've got to do what the *Memsahib* tells me.
Would you believe that the man she hired it
from tells me that all four of the men—they were
brothers—died of cholera on the way to Hard-
war, poor devils; and the 'rickshaw has been
broken up by the man himself. 'Told me he
never used a dead *Memsahib's* 'rickshaw. 'Spoiled
his luck. Queer notion, wasn't it? Fancy poor
little Mrs. Wessington spoiling any one's luck
except her own!" I laughed aloud at this point;
and my laugh jarred on me as I uttered it. So
there *were* ghosts of 'rickshaws after all, and
ghostly employments in the other world! How
much did Mrs. Wessington give her men? What
were their hours? Where did they go?

And for visible answer to my last question I
saw the infernal Thing blocking my path in the

twilight. The dead travel fast, and by short cuts
unknown to ordinary coolies. I laughed aloud a
second time and checked my laughter suddenly,
for I was afraid I was going mad. Mad to a
certain extent I must have been, for I recollect
that I reined in my horse at the head of the 'rickshaw, and politely wished Mrs. Wessington
"Good-evening." Her answer was one I knew
only too well. I listened to the end; and replied
that I had heard it all before, but should be delighted if she had anything further to say. Some
malignant devil stronger than I must have entered into me that evening, for I have a dim recollection of talking the commonplaces of the
day for five minutes to the Thing in front of me.

"Mad as a hatter, poor devil—or drunk. Max,
try and get him to come home."

Surely *that* was not Mrs. Wessington's voice!
The two men had overheard me speaking to the
empty air, and had returned to look after me.
They were very kind and considerate, and from
their words evidently gathered that I was extremely drunk. I thanked them confusedly and
cantered away to my hotel, there changed, and
arrived at the Mannerings' ten minutes late. I
pleaded the darkness of the night as an excuse;
was rebuked by Kitty for my unlover-like tardi-
ness; and sat down.

The conversation had already become general;

and under cover of it, I was addressing some
tender small talk to my sweetheart when I was
aware that at the further end of the table a short
red-whiskered man was describing, with much
broidery, his encounter with a mad unknown
that evening.

A few sentences convinced me that he was repeating the incident of half an hour ago. In the
middle of the story he looked round for applause,
as professional story-tellers do, caught my eye,
and straightway collapsed. There was a moment's awkward silence, and the red-whiskered
man muttered something to the effect that he
had "forgotten the rest," thereby sacrificing a
reputation as a good story-teller which he had
built up for six seasons past. I blessed him
from the bottom of my heart, and—went on
with my fish.

In the fulness of time that dinner came to an
end; and with genuine regret I tore myself away
from Kitty—as certain as I was of my own existence that It would be waiting for me outside
the door. The red-whiskered man, who had
been introduced to me as Doctor Heatherlegh of
Simla, volunteered to bear me company as far as
our roads lay together. I accepted his offer with
gratitude.

My instinct had not deceived me. It lay in
readiness in the Mall, and, in what seemed devil-

ish mockery of our ways, with a lighted head-
lamp. The red-whiskered man went to the
point at once, in a manner that showed he had
been thinking over it all dinner time.

"I say, Pansay, what the deuce was the matter with you this evening on the Elysium road?'
The suddenness of the question wrenched an answer from me before I was aware.

"That!" said I, pointing to It.

" *That* may be either D. T. or Eyes for aught I
know. Now you don't liquor. I saw as much
at dinner, so it can't be *D. T.* There's nothing
whatever where you're pointing, though you're
sweating and trembling with fright like a scared
pony. Therefore, I conclude that it's Eyes. And
I ought to understand all about them. Come
along home with me. I'm on the Blessington
lower road."

To my intense delight the 'rickshaw instead of
waiting for us kept about twenty yards ahead—
and this, too, whether we walked, trotted, or
cantered. In the course of that long night ride I
had told my companion almost as much as I have
told you here.

"Well, you've spoiled one of the best tales
I've ever laid tongue to," said he, "but I'll forgive you for the sake of what you've gone
through. Now come home and do what I tell
you; and when I've cured you, young man, let

this be a lesson to you to steer clear of women and indigestible food till the day of your death."

The 'rickshaw kept steady in front; and my red-whiskered friend seemed to derive great pleasure from my account of its exact whereabouts.

"Eyes, Pansay—all Eyes, Brain, and Stomach. And the greatest of these three is Stomach. You've too much conceited Brain, too little Stomach, and thoroughly unhealthy Eyes. Get your Stomach straight and the rest follows. And all that's French for a liver pill. I'll take sole medical charge of you from this hour! for you're too interesting a phenomenon to be passed over."

By this time we were deep in the shadow of the Blessington lower road and the 'rickshaw came to a dead stop under a pine-clad, overhanging shale cliff. Instinctively I halted too, giving my reason. Heatherlegh rapped out an oath.

"Now, if you think I'm going to spend a cold night on the hillside for the sake of a Stomach-*cum*-Brain-*cum*-Eye illusion . . . Lord, ha' mercy! What's that?"

There was a muffled report, a blinding smother of dust just in front of us, a crack, the noise of rent boughs, and about ten yards of the cliff-side —pines, undergrowth, and all—slid down into the road below, completely blocking it up. The uprooted trees swayed and tottered for a moment like drunken giants in the gloom, and then fell prone among their fellows with a thunderous crash. Our two horses stood motionless and sweating with fear. As soon as the rattle of falling earth and stone had subsided, my companion muttered:—"Man, if we'd gone forward we should have been ten feet deep in our graves by now. 'There are more things in heaven and earth.' . . . Come home, Pansay, and thank God. I want a peg badly."

We retraced our way over the Church Ridge, and I arrived at Dr. Heatherlegh's house shortly after midnight.

His attempts toward my cure commenced almost immediately, and for a week I never left his sight. Many a time in the course of that week did I bless the good-fortune which had thrown me in contact with Simla's best and kindest doctor. Day by day my spirits grew lighter and more equable. Day by day, too, I became more and more inclined to fall in with Heatherlegh's "spectral illusion" theory, implicating eyes, brain, and stomach. I wrote to Kitty, telling her that a slight sprain caused by a fall from my horse kept me indoors for a few days; and that I should be recovered before she had time to regret my absence.

Heatherlegh's treatment was simple to a degree. It consisted of liver pills, cold-water baths, and strong exercise, taken in the dusk or at early dawn—for, as he sagely observed:—"A man with a sprained ankle doesn't walk a dozen miles a day, and your young woman might be wondering if she saw you."

At the end of the week, after much examination of pupil and pulse, and strict injunctions as to diet and pedestrianism, Heatherlegh dismissed me as brusquely as he had taken charge of me. Here is his parting benediction:—"Man, I certify to your mental cure, and that's as much as to say I've cured most of your bodily ailments. Now, get your traps out of this as soon as you can; and be off to make love to Miss Kitty."

I was endeavoring to express my thanks for his kindness. He cut me short.

"Don't think I did this because I like you. I gather that you've behaved like a blackguard all through. But, all the same, you're a phenomenon, and as queer a phenomenon as you are a blackguard. No!"—checking me a second time —"not a rupee please. Go out and see if you can find the eyes-brain-and-stomach business again. I'll give you a lakh for each time you see it."

Half an hour later I was in the Mannerings' drawing-room with Kitty—drunk with the in-

toxication of present happiness and the fore-
knowledge that I should never more be troubled
with Its hideous presence. Strong in the sense
of my new-found security, I proposed a ride
at once; and, by preference, a canter round
Jakko.

Never had I felt so well, so overladen with
vitality and mere animal spirits, as I did on the
afternoon of the 30th of April. Kitty was delighted at the change in my appearance, and
complimented me on it in her delightfully frank
and outspoken manner. We left the Mannerings' house together, laughing and talking, and
cantered along the Chota Simla road as of old.

I was in haste to reach the Sanjowlie Reservoir
and there make my assurance doubly sure. The
horses did their best, but seemed all too slow to
my impatient mind. Kitty was astonished at my
boisterousness. "Why, Jack!" she cried at last,
"you are behaving like a child. What are you
doing?"

We were just below the Convent, and from
sheer wantonness I was making my Waler
plunge and curvet across the road as I tickled it
with the loop of my riding-whip.

"Doing?" I answered; "nothing, dear.
That's just it. If you'd been doing nothing
for a week except lie up, you'd be as riotous
as I.

> "'Singing and murmuring in your feastful mirth,
>   Joying to feel yourself alive;
>   Lord over Nature, Lord of the visible Earth,
>   Lord of the senses five.'"

My quotation was hardly out of my lips before we had rounded the corner above the Convent; and a few yards further on could see across to Sanjowlie. In the centre of the level road stood the black and white liveries, the yellow-paneled 'rickshaw, and Mrs. Keith-Wessington. I pulled up, looked, rubbed my eyes, and, I believe, must have said something. The next thing I knew was that I was lying face downward on the road, with Kitty kneeling above me in tears.

"Has it gone, child!" I gasped. Kitty only wept more bitterly.

"Has what gone, Jack dear? what does it all mean? There must be a mistake somewhere, Jack. A hideous mistake." Her last words brought me to my feet—mad—raving for the time being.

"Yes, there *is* a mistake somewhere," I repeated, "a hideous mistake. Come and look at It."

I have an indistinct idea that I dragged Kitty by the wrist along the road up to where It stood, and implored her for pity's sake to speak to It; to tell It that we were betrothed; that neither Death nor Hell could break the tie between us:

and Kitty only knows how much more to the
same effect. Now and again I appealed passion-
ately to the Terror in the 'rickshaw to bear witness to all I had said, and to release me from a
torture that was killing me. As I talked I suppose I must have told Kitty of my old relations
with Mrs. Wessington, for I saw her listen intently with white face and blazing eyes.

"Thank you, Mr. Pansay," she said, "that's
quite enough. *Syce ghora láo.*"

The syces, impassive as Orientals always are,
had come up with the recaptured horses; and as
Kitty sprang into her saddle I caught hold of the
bridle, entreating her to hear me out and forgive. My answer was the cut of her riding-
whip across my face from mouth to eye, and a
word or two of farewell that even now I cannot
write down. So I judged, and judged rightly,
that Kitty knew all; and I staggered back to the
side of the 'rickshaw. My face was cut and
bleeding, and the blow of the riding-whip had
raised a livid blue wheal on it. I had no self-
respect. Just then, Heatherlegh, who must have
been following Kitty and me at a distance, cantered up.

"Doctor," I said, pointing to my face, "here's
Miss Mannering's signature to my order of dis-
missal and . . . I'll thank you for that lakh
as soon as convenient."

Heatherlegh's face, even in my abject misery, moved me to laughter.

"I'll stake my professional reputation"—he began. "Don't be a fool," I whispered. "I've lost my life's happiness and you'd better take me home."

As I spoke the 'rickshaw was gone. Then I lost all knowledge of what was passing. The crest of Jakko seemed to heave and roll like the crest of a cloud and fall in upon me.

Seven days later (on the 7th of May, that is to say) I was aware that I was lying in Heatherlegh's room as weak as a little child. Heatherlegh was watching me intently from behind the papers on his writing-table. His first words were not encouraging; but I was too far spent to be much moved by them.

"Here's Miss Kitty has sent back your letters. You corresponded a good deal, you young people. Here's a packet that looks like a ring, and a cheerful sort of a note from Mannering Papa, which I've taken the liberty of reading and burning. The old gentleman's not pleased with you."

"And Kitty?" I asked, dully.

"Rather more drawn than her father from what she says. By the same token you must have been letting out any number of queer reminiscences just before I met you. 'Says that a man who would have behaved to a woman as

you did to Mrs. Wessington ought to kill himself out of sheer pity for his kind. She's a hot-
headed little virago, your mash. 'Will have it
too that you were suffering from *D. T.* when that
row on the Jakko road turned up. 'Says she'll
die before she ever speaks to you again."

I groaned and turned over on the other side.

"Now you've got your choice, my friend.
This engagement has to be broken off; and the
Mannerings don't want to be too hard on you.
Was it broken through *D. T.* or epileptic fits?
Sorry I can't offer you a better exchange unless
you'd prefer hereditary insanity. Say the word
and I'll tell 'em it's fits. All Simla knows about
that scene on the Ladies' Mile. Come! I'll give
you five minutes to think over it."

During those five minutes I believe that I ex-
plored thoroughly the lowest circles of the In-
ferno which it is permitted man to tread on earth.
And at the same time I myself was watching
myself faltering through the dark labyrinths of
doubt, misery, and utter despair. I wondered, as
Heatherlegh in his chair might have wondered,
which dreadful alternative I should adopt. Presently I heard myself answering in a voice that I
hardly recognized,—

"They're confoundedly particular about morality in these parts. Give 'em fits, Heatherlegh,
and my love. Now let me sleep a bit longer."

Then my two selves joined, and it was only I
(half crazed, devil-driven I) that tossed in my
bed, tracing step by step the history of the past
month.

"But I am in Simla," I kept repeating to myself. "I, Jack Pansay, am in Simla, and there
are no ghosts here. It's unreasonable of that
woman to pretend there are. Why couldn't
Agnes have left me alone? I never did her any
harm. It might just as well have been me as
Agnes. Only I'd never have come back on pur-
pose to kill *her*. Why can't I be left alone—left
alone and happy?"

It was high noon when I first awoke: and the
sun was low in the sky before I slept—slept as
the tortured criminal sleeps on his rack, too worn
to feel further pain.

Next day I could not leave my bed. Heatherlegh told me in the morning that he had received
an answer from Mr. Mannering, and that, thanks
to his (Heatherlegh's) friendly offices, the story
of my affliction had traveled through the length
and breadth of Simla, where I was on all sides
much pitied.

"And that's rather more than you deserve," he
concluded, pleasantly, "though the Lord knows
you've been going through a pretty severe mill.
Never mind; we'll cure you yet, you perverse
phenomenon."

I declined firmly to be cured. "You've been much too good to me already, old man," said I; "but I don't think I need trouble you further."

In my heart I knew that nothing Heatherlegh could do would lighten the burden that had been laid upon me.

With that knowledge came also a sense of hopeless, impotent rebellion against the unreasonableness of it all. There were scores of men no better than I whose punishments had at least been reserved for another world; and I felt that it was bitterly, cruelly unfair that I alone should have been singled out for so hideous a fate. This mood would in time give place to another where it seemed that the 'rickshaw and I were the only realities in a world of shadows; that Kitty was a ghost; that Mannering, Heatherlegh, and all the other men and women I knew were all ghosts; and the great, grey hills themselves but vain shadows devised to torture me. From mood to mood I tossed backward and forward for seven weary days; my body growing daily stronger and stronger, until the bedroom looking-glass told me that I had returned to everyday life, and was as other men once more. Curiously enough my face showed no signs of the struggle I had gone through. It was pale indeed, but as expressionless and commonplace as ever. I had expected some permanent alteration—visible evi-

dence of the disease that was eating me away.
I found nothing.

On the 15th of May I left Heatherlegh's house
at eleven o'clock in the morning; and the instinct
of the bachelor drove me to the Club. There I
found that every man knew my story as told by
Heatherlegh, and was, in clumsy fashion, abnor-
mally kind and attentive. Nevertheless I recognized that for the rest of my natural life I should
be among but not of my fellows; and I envied
very bitterly indeed the laughing coolies on the
Mall below. I lunched at the Club, and at four
o'clock wandered aimlessly down the Mall in the
vague hope of meeting Kitty. Close to the
Band-stand the black and white liveries joined
me; and I heard Mrs. Wessington's old appeal at
my side. I had been expecting this ever since I
came out; and was only surprised at her delay.
The phantom 'rickshaw and I went side by side
along the Chota Simla road in silence. Close to
the bazar, Kitty and a man on horseback over-
took and passed us. For any sign she gave I
might have been a dog in the road. She did not
even pay me the compliment of quickening her
pace; though the rainy afternoon had served for
an excuse.

So Kitty and her companion, and I and my
ghostly Light-o'-Love, crept round Jakko in
couples. The road was streaming with water;

the pines dripped like roof-pipes on the rocks below, and the air was full of fine, driving rain.
Two or three times I found myself saying to myself almost aloud: "I'm Jack Pansay on leave at
Simla—*at Simla!* Everyday, ordinary Simla. I
mustn't forget that—I mustn't forget that." Then
I would try to recollect some of the gossip I had
heard at the Club: the prices of So-and-So's
horses—anything, in fact, that related to the
workaday Anglo-Indian world I knew so well.
I even repeated the multiplication-table rapidly to
myself, to make quite sure that I was not taking
leave of my senses. It gave me much comfort;
and must have prevented my hearing Mrs. Wessington for a time.

Once more I wearily climbed the Convent
slope and entered the level road. Here Kitty
and the man started off at a canter, and I was
left alone with Mrs. Wessington. "Agnes,"
said I, "will you put back your hood and tell
me what it all means?" The hood dropped
noiselessly, and I was face to face with my
dead and buried mistress. She was wearing
the dress in which I had last seen her alive;
carried the same tiny handkerchief in her right
hand; and the same cardcase in her left. (A
woman eight months dead with a cardcase!) I
had to pin myself down to the multiplication-
table, and to set both hands on the stone parapet

of the road, to assure myself that that at least was real.

"Agnes," I repeated, "for pity's sake tell me what it all means." Mrs. Wessington leaned forward, with that odd, quick turn of the head I used to know so well, and spoke.

If my story had not already so madly over-leaped the bounds of all human belief I should apologize to you now. As I know that no one —no, not even Kitty, for whom it is written as some sort of justification of my conduct—will believe me, I will go on. Mrs. Wessington spoke and I walked with her from the Sanjowlie road to the turning below the Commander-in-Chief's house as I might walk by the side of any living woman's 'rickshaw, deep in conversation. The second and most tormenting of my moods of sickness had suddenly laid hold upon me, and like the Prince in Tennyson's poem, "I seemed to move amid a world of ghosts." There had been a garden-party at the Commander-in-Chief's, and we two joined the crowd of home-ward-bound folk. As I saw them then it seemed that *they* were the shadows—impalpable, fantastic shadows—that divided for Mrs. Wessington's 'rickshaw to pass through. What we said during the course of that weird interview I cannot —indeed, I dare not—tell. Heatherlegh's comment would have been a short laugh and a remark that I had been "mashing a brain-eye-and-stomach chimera." It was a ghastly and yet in some indefinable way a marvelously dear experience. Could it be possible, I wondered, that I was in this life to woo a second time the woman I had killed by my own neglect and cruelty?

I met Kitty on the homeward road—a shadow among shadows.

If I were to describe all the incidents of the next fortnight in their order, my story would never come to an end; and your patience would be exhausted. Morning after morning and evening after evening the ghostly 'rickshaw and I used to wander through Simla together. Wherever I went there the four black and white liveries followed me and bore me company to and from my hotel. At the Theatre I found them amid the crowd of yelling *jhampanies;* outside the Club veranda, after a long evening of whist; at the Birthday Ball, waiting patiently for my re-appearance; and in broad daylight when I went calling. Save that it cast no shadow, the 'rickshaw was in every respect as real to look upon as one of wood and iron. More than once, indeed, I have had to check myself from warning some hard-riding friend against cantering over it. More than once I have walked down the Mall deep in conversation with Mrs. Wessington to the unspeakable amazement of the passers-by.

Before I had been out and about a week I learned that the "fit" theory had been discarded in favor of insanity. However, I made no change in my mode of life. I called, rode, and dined out as freely as ever. I had a passion for the society of my kind which I had never felt before; I hungered to be among the realities of life; and at the same time I felt vaguely unhappy when I had been separated too long from my ghostly companion. It would be almost impossible to describe my varying moods from the 15th of May up to to-day.

The presence of the 'rickshaw filled me by turns with horror, blind fear, a dim sort of pleasure, and utter despair. I dared not leave Simla; and I knew that my stay there was killing me. I knew, moreover, that it was my destiny to die slowly and a little every day. My only anxiety was to get the penance over as quietly as might be. Alternately I hungered for a sight of Kitty and watched her outrageous flirtations with my successor—to speak more accurately, my successors—with amused interest. She was as much out of my life as I was out of hers. By day I wandered with Mrs. Wessington almost content. By night I implored Heaven to let me return to the world as I used to know it. Above all these varying moods lay the sensation of dull, numbing wonder that the Seen and the Unseen should

mingle so strangely on this earth to hound one
poor soul to its grave.

*   *   *   *   *   *

August 27.—Heatherlegh has been indefatiga-
ble in his attendance on me; and only yesterday
told me that I ought to send in an application for
sick leave. An application to escape the company of a phantom! A request that the Government would graciously permit me to get rid of
five ghosts and an airy 'rickshaw by going to
England! Heatherlegh's proposition moved me
to almost hysterical laughter. I told him that I
should await the end quietly at Simla; and I am
sure that the end is not far off. Believe me that
I dread its advent more than any word can say;
and I torture myself nightly with a thousand
speculations as to the manner of my death.

Shall I die in my bed decently and as an English gentleman should die; or, in one last walk
on the Mall, will my soul be wrenched from me
to take its place forever and ever by the side of
that ghastly phantasm ? Shall I return to my old
lost allegiance in the next world, or shall I meet
Agnes loathing her and bound to her side through
all eternity ? Shall we two hover over the scene
of our lives till the end of Time ? As the day of
my death draws nearer, the intense horror that
all living flesh feels toward escaped spirits from

beyond the grave grows more and more power-
ful. It is an awful thing to go down quick
among the dead with scarcely one-half of your
life completed. It is a thousand times more
awful to wait as I do in your midst, for I know
not what unimaginable terror. Pity me, at least
on the score of my "delusion," for I know you
will never believe what I have written here. Yet
as surely as ever a man was done to death by the
Powers of Darkness I am that man.

In justice, too, pity her. For as surely as ever
woman was killed by man, I killed Mrs. Wessington. And the last portion of my punishment
is even now upon me.

MY OWN TRUE GHOST STORY

MY OWN TRUE GHOST STORY

As I came through the Desert thus it was—
As I came through the Desert.
—*The City of Dreadful Night.*

SOMEWHERE in the Other World, where there are books and pictures and plays and shop-windows to look at, and thousands of men who spend their lives in building up all four, lives a gentleman who writes real stories about the real insides of people; and his name is Mr. Walter Besant. But he will insist upon treating his ghosts — he has published half a workshopful of them—with levity. He makes his ghost-seers talk familiarly, and, in some cases, flirt outrageously, with the phantoms. You may treat anything, from a Viceroy to a Vernacular Paper, with levity; but you must behave reverently toward a ghost, and particularly an Indian one.

There are, in this land, ghosts who take the form of fat, cold, pobby corpses, and hide in trees near the roadside till a traveler passes. Then they drop upon his neck and remain. There are also terrible ghosts of women who have died in child-bed. These wander along the pathways at dusk, or hide in the crops near a village, and call seductively. But to answer their call is death in this world and the next. Their feet are turned backward that all sober men may recognize them. There are ghosts of little children who have been thrown into wells. These haunt well-curbs and the fringes of jungles, and wail under the stars, or catch women by the wrist and beg to be taken up and carried. These and the corpse-ghosts, however, are only vernacular articles and do not attack Sahibs. No native ghost has yet been authentically reported to have frightened an Englishman; but many English ghosts have scared the life out of both white and black.

Nearly every other Station owns a ghost. There are said to be two at Simla, not counting the woman who blows the bellows at Syree dâk-bungalow on the Old Road; Mussoorie has a house haunted of a very lively Thing; a White Lady is supposed to do night-watchman round a house in Lahore; Dalhousie says that one of her houses "repeats" on autumn evenings all the incidents of a horrible horse-and-precipice accident; Murree has a merry ghost, and, now that she has been swept by cholera, will have room for a sorrowful one; there are Officers' Quarters in Mian Mir whose doors open without reason, and whose furniture is guaranteed to creak, not

with the heat of June but with the weight of In-
visibles who come to lounge in the chair; Peshawur possesses houses that none will willingly
rent; and there is something—not fever—wrong
with a big bungalow in Allahabad. The older
Provinces simply bristle with haunted houses,
and march phantom armies along their main
thoroughfares.

Some of the dâk-bungalows on the Grand
Trunk Road have handy little cemeteries in their
compound—witnesses to the "changes and
chances of this mortal life" in the days when
men drove from Calcutta to the Northwest.
These bungalows are objectionable places to put
up in. They are generally very old, lways
dirty, while the *khansamah* is as ancient as the
bungalow. He either chatters senilely, or falls
into the long trances of age. In both moods he
is useless. If you get angry with him, he refers
to some Sahib dead and buried these thirty years,
and says that when he was in that Sahib's service
not a *khansamah* in the Province could touch
him. Then he jabbers and mows and trembles
and fidgets among the dishes, and you repent of
your irritation.

In these dâk-bungalows, ghosts are most likely
to be found, and when found, they should be
made a note of. Not long ago it was my business to live in dâk-bungalows. I never inhabited

the same house for three nights running, and grew to be learned in the breed. I lived in Government-built ones with red brick walls and rail ceilings, an inventory of the furniture posted in every room, and an excited snake at the threshold to give welcome. I lived in "converted" ones—old houses officiating as dâk-bungalows—where nothing was in its proper place and there wasn't even a fowl for dinner. I lived in second-hand palaces where the wind blew through open-work marble tracery just as uncomfortably as through a broken pane. I lived in dâk-bungalows where the last entry in the visitors' book was fifteen months old, and where they s ..shed off the curry-kid's head with a sword. It was my good-luck to meet all sorts of men, from sober traveling missionaries and deserters flying from British Regiments, to drunken loafers who threw whiskey bottles at all who passed; and my still greater good-fortune just to escape a maternity case. Seeing that a fair proportion of the tragedy of our lives out here acted itself in dâk-bungalows, I wondered that I had met no ghosts. A ghost that would voluntarily hang about a dâk-bungalow would be mad of course; but so many men have died mad in dâk-bungalows that there must be a fair percentage of lunatic ghosts.

In due time I found my ghost, or ghosts rather.

for there were two of them. Up till that hour I had sympathized with Mr. Besant's method of handling them, as shown in " *The Strange Case of Mr. Lucraft and other Stories.*" I am now in the Opposition.

We will call the bungalow Katmal dâk-bungalow. But *that* was the smallest part of the horror. A man with a sensitive hide has no right to sleep in dâk-bungalows. He should marry. Katmal dâk-bungalow was old and rotten and unrepaired. The floor was of worn brick, the walls were filthy, and the windows were nearly black with grime. It stood on a by-path largely used by native Sub-Deputy Assistants of all kinds, from Finance to Forests; but real Sahibs were rare. The *khansamah*, who was nearly bent double with old age, said so.

When I arrived, there was a fitful, undecided rain on the face of the land, accompanied by a restless wind, and every gust made a noise like the rattling of dry bones in the stiff toddy-palms outside. The *khansamah* completely lost his head on my arrival. He had served a Sahib once. Did I know that Sahib? He gave me the name of a well-known man who has been buried for more than a quarter of a century, and showed me an ancient daguerreotype of that man in his prehistoric youth. I had seen a steel engraving of him at the head of a double volume of Memoirs a month before, and I felt ancient beyond telling.

The day shut in and the *khansamah* went to get me food. He did not go through the pretence of calling it "*khana*"—man's victuals. He said "*ratub*," and that means, among other things, "grub"—dog's rations. There was no insult in his choice of the term. He had forgotten the other word, I suppose.

While he was cutting up the dead bodies of animals, I settled myself down, after exploring the dâk-bungalow. There were three rooms, beside my own, which was a corner kennel, each giving into the other through dingy white doors fastened with long iron bars. The bungalow was a very solid one, but the partition-walls of the rooms were almost jerry-built in their flimsiness. Every step or bang of a trunk echoed from my room down the other three, and every footfall came back tremulously from the far walls. For this reason I shut the door. There were no lamps—only candles in long glass shades. An oil wick was set in the bath-room.

For bleak, unadulterated misery that dâk-bungalow was the worst of the many that I had ever set foot in. There was no fireplace, and the windows would not open; so a brazier of charcoal would have been useless. The rain and the wind splashed and gurgled and moaned round the house, and the toddy-palms rattled and roared. Half a dozen jackals went through the compound singing, and a hyena stood afar off and mocked them. A hyena would convince a Sadducee of the Resurrection of the Dead—the worst sort of Dead. Then came the *ratub*—a curious meal, half native and half English in composition—with the old *khansamah* babbling behind my chair about dead and gone English people, and the wind-blown candles playing shadow-bo-peep with the bed and the mosquito-curtains. It was just the sort of dinner and evening to make a man think of every single one of his past sins, and of all the others that he intended to commit if he lived.

Sleep, for several hundred reasons, was not easy. The lamp in the bath-room threw the most absurd shadows into the room, and the wind was beginning to talk nonsense.

Just when the reasons were drowsy with blood-sucking I heard the regular—" Let-us-take-and-heave-him-over" grunt of doolie-bearers in the compound. First one doolie came in, then a second, and then a third. I heard the doolies dumped on the ground, and the shutter in front of my door shook. "That's some one trying to come in," I said. But no one spoke, and I per-suaded myself that it was the gusty wind. The shutter of the room next to mine was attacked, flung back, and the inner door opened. " That's some Sub-Deputy Assistant," I said, " and he has brought his friends with him. Now they'll talk and spit and smoke for an hour."

But there were no voices and no footsteps. No one was putting his luggage into the next room. The door shut, and I thanked Providence that I was to be left in peace. But I was curious to know where the doolies had gone. I got out of bed and looked into the darkness. There was never a sign of a doolie. Just as I was getting into bed again, I heard, in the next room, the sound that no man in his senses can possibly mistake—the whir of a billiard ball down the length of the slates when the striker is stringing for break. No other sound is like it. A minute afterward there was another whir, and I got into bed. I was not frightened—indeed I was not. I was very curious to know what had become of the doolies. I jumped into bed for that reason.

Next minute I heard the double click of a cannon and my hair sat up. It is a mistake to say that hair stands up. The skin of the head tightens and you can feel a faint, prickly bristling all over the scalp. That is the hair sitting up.

There was a whir and a click, and both sounds could only have been made by one thing—a billiard ball. I argued the matter out at great length with myself; and the more I argued the less probable it seemed that one bed, one table, and two chairs—all the furniture of the room next to mine—could so exactly duplicate the sounds of a game of billiards. After another cannon, a three-cushion one to judge by the whir, I argued no more. I had found my ghost and would have given worlds to have escaped from that dâk-bungalow. I listened, and with each listen the game grew clearer. There was whir on whir and click on click. Sometimes there was a double click and a whir and another click. Beyond any sort of doubt, people were playing billiards in the next room. And the next room was not big enough to hold a billiard table!

Between the pauses of the wind I heard the game go forward—stroke after stroke. I tried to believe that I could not hear voices; but that attempt was a failure.

Do you know what fear is? Not ordinary fear of insult, injury or death, but abject, quivering dread of something that you cannot see—fear that dries the inside of the mouth and half of the throat—fear that makes you sweat on the palms of the hands, and gulp in order to keep the uvula at work? This is a fine Fear—a great cowardice, and must be felt to be appreciated. The very improbability of billiards in a dâk-bungalow proved the reality of the thing. No man—drunk or sober—could imagine a game at billiards, or invent the spitting crack of a "screw-cannon."

A severe course of dâk-bungalows has this disadvantage—it breeds infinite credulity. If a man said to a confirmed dâk-bungalow-haunter: —"There is a corpse in the next room, and there's a mad girl in the next but one, and the woman and man on that camel have just eloped from a place sixty miles away," the hearer would not disbelieve because he would know that nothing is too wild, grotesque, or horrible to happen in a dâk-bungalow.

This credulity, unfortunately, extends to ghosts. A rational person fresh from his own house would have turned on his side and slept. I did not. So surely as I was given up as a bad carcass by the scores of things in the bed because the bulk of my blood was in my heart, so surely did I hear every stroke of a long game at billiards played in the echoing room behind the iron-barred door. My dominant fear was that the players might want a maker. It was an absurd fear; because creatures who could play in the dark would be above such superfluities. I only know that that was my terror; and it was real.

After a long long while, the game stopped, and the door banged. I slept because I was dead tired. Otherwise I should have preferred to have kept awake. Not for everything in Asia would I have dropped the door-bar and peered into the dark of the next room.

When the morning came, I considered that I had done well and wisely, and inquired for the means of departure.

"By the way, *khansamah*," I said, "what were those three doolies doing in my compound in the night?"

"There were no doolies," said the *khansamah.*

I went into the next room and the daylight streamed through the open door. I was immensely brave. I would, at that hour, have played Black Pool with the owner of the big Black Pool down below.

"Has this place always been a dâk-bungalow?" I asked.

"No," said the *khansamah.* "Ten or twenty years ago, I have forgotten how long, it was a billiard-room."

"A how much?"

"A billiard-room for the Sahibs who built the Railway. I was *khansamah* then in the big house where all the Railway-Sahibs lived, and I used to come across with brandy-*shrab.* These three rooms were all one, and they held a big table on which the Sahibs played every evening. But the Sahibs are all dead now, and the Railway runs, you say, nearly to Kabul."

"Do you remember anything about the Sahibs?"

"It is long ago, but I remember that one Sahib, a fat man and always angry, was playing here one night, and he said to me:—'Mangal Khan, brandy-*pani do*,' and I filled the glass, and he bent over the table to strike, and his head fell lower and lower till it hit the table, and his spectacles came off, and when we—the Sahibs and I myself—ran to lift him he was dead. I helped to carry him out. Aha, he was a strong Sahib! But he is dead and I, old Mangal Khan, am still living, by your favor."

That was more than enough! I had my ghost —a first-hand, authenticated article. I would write to the Society for Psychical Research—I would paralyze the Empire with the news! But I would, first of all, put eighty miles of assessed crop-land between myself and that dâk-bunga-low before nightfall. The Society might send their regular agent to investigate later on.

I went into my own room and prepared to pack after noting down the facts of the case. As I smoked I heard the game begin again—with a miss in balk this time, for the whir was a short one.

The door was open and I could see into the room. *Click—click!* That was a cannon. I entered the room without fear, for there was

sunlight within and a fresh breeze without. The
unseen game was going on at a tremendous rate.
And well it might, when a restless little rat was
running to and fro inside the dingy ceiling-cloth,
and a piece of loose window-sash was making
fifty breaks off the window-bolt as it shook in
the breeze!

Impossible to mistake the sound of billiard
balls! Impossible to mistake the whir of a ball
over the slate! But I was to be excused. Even
when I shut my enlightened eyes the sound was
marvelously like that of a fast game.

Entered angrily the faithful partner of my sor-
rows, Kadir Baksh.

"This bungalow is very bad and low-caste!
No wonder the Presence was disturbed and is
speckled. Three sets of doolie-bearers came to
the bungalow late last night when I was sleeping
outside, and said that it was their custom to rest
in the rooms set apart for the English people!
What honor has the *khansamah*? They tried to
enter, but I told them to go. No wonder, if
these *Oorias* have been here, that the Presence is
sorely spotted. It is shame, and the work of a
dirty man!"

Kadir Baksh did not say that he had taken
from each gang two annas for rent in advance,
and then, beyond my earshot, had beaten them
with the big green umbrella whose use I could

never before divine. But Kadir Baksh has no notions of morality.

There was an interview with the *khansamah*, but as he promptly lost his head, wrath gave place to pity, and pity led to a long conversation, in the course of which he put the fat Engineer-Sahib's tragic death in three separate stations—two of them fifty miles away. The third shift was to Calcutta, and there the Sahib died while driving a dog-cart.

If I had encouraged him the *khansamah* would have wandered all through Bengal with his corpse.

I did not go away as soon as I intended. I stayed for the night, while the wind and the rat and the sash and the window-bolt played a ding-dong "hundred and fifty up." Then the wind ran out and the billiards stopped, and I felt that I had ruined my one genuine, hall-marked ghost story.

Had I only stopped at the proper time, I could have made *anything* out of it.

That was the bitterest thought of all!

THE STRANGE RIDE OF MORROWBIE JUKES

THE STRANGE RIDE OF MOR-
ROWBIE JUKES

Alive or dead—there is no other way.—Native Proverb.

THERE is, as the conjurers say, no deception
about this tale. Jukes by accident stum-
bled upon a village that is well known to exist,
though he is the only Englishman who has been
there. A somewhat similar institution used to
flourish on the outskirts of Calcutta, and there is
a story that if you go into the heart of Bikanir,
which is in the heart of the Great Indian Desert,
you shall come across not a village but a town
where the Dead who did not die but may not
live have established their headquarters. And,
since it is perfectly true that in the same Desert
is a wonderful city where all the rich money-
lenders retreat after they have made their fortunes (fortunes so vast that the owners cannot
trust even the strong hand of the Government to
protect them, but take refuge in the waterless
sands), and drive sumptuous C-spring barouches,
and buy beautiful girls and decorate their palaces
with gold and ivory and Minton tiles and mother-
o'-pearl, I do not see why Jukes's tale should not

be true.   He is a Civil Engineer, with a head for
plans and distances and things of that kind, and
he certainly would not take the trouble to invent
imaginary traps.   He could earn more by doing
his legitimate work.   He never varies the tale in
the telling, and grows very hot and indignant
when he thinks of the disrespectful treatment he
received.   He wrote this quite straightforwardly
at first, but he has since touched it up in places
and introduced Moral Reflections, thus:

In the beginning it all arose from a slight attack of fever.   My work necessitated my being
in camp for some months between Pakpattan
and Mubarakpur—a desolate sandy stretch of
country as every one who has had the misfortune to go there may know.   My coolies were
neither more nor less exasperating than other
gangs, and my work demanded sufficient attention to keep me from moping, had I been inclined to so unmanly a weakness.

On the 23d December, 1884, I felt a little feverish.   There was a full moon at the time, and, in
consequence, every dog near my tent was baying
it.   The brutes assembled in twos and threes and
drove me frantic.   A few days previously I had
shot one loud-mouthed singer and suspended his
carcass *in terrorem* about fifty yards from my
tent-door.   But his friends fell upon, fought for,

and ultimately devoured the body: and, as it seemed to me, sang their hymns of thanksgiving afterward with renewed energy.

The light-headedness which accompanies fever acts differently on different men. My irritation gave way, after a short time, to a fixed determination to slaughter one huge black and white beast who had been foremost in song and first in flight throughout the evening. Thanks to a shaking hand and a giddy head I had already missed him twice with both barrels of my shotgun, when it struck me that my best plan would be to ride him down in the open and finish him off with a hog-spear. This, of course, was merely the semi-delirious notion of a fever patient; but I remember that it struck me at the time as being eminently practical and feasible.

I therefore ordered my groom to saddle Pornic and bring him round quietly to the rear of my tent. When the pony was ready, I stood at his head prepared to mount and dash out as soon as the dog should again lift up his voice. Pornic, by the way, had not been out of his pickets for a couple of days; the night air was crisp and chilly; and I was armed with a specially long and sharp pair of persuaders with which I had been rousing a sluggish cob that afternoon. You will easily believe, then, that when he was let go he went quickly. In one moment, for the brute bolted as straight as a die, the tent was left far behind, and we were flying over the smooth sandy soil at racing speed. In another we had passed the wretched dog, and I had almost forgotten why it was that I had taken horse and hog-spear.

The delirium of fever and the excitement of rapid motion through the air must have taken away the remnant of my senses. I have a faint recollection of standing upright in my stirrups, and of brandishing my hog-spear at the great white Moon that looked down so calmly on my mad gallop; and of shouting challenges to the camel-thorn bushes as they whizzed past. Once or twice, I believe, I swayed forward on Pornic's neck, and literally hung on by my spurs—as the marks next morning showed.

The wretched beast went forward like a thing possessed, over what seemed to be a limitless expanse of moonlit sand. Next, I remember, the ground rose suddenly in front of us, and as we topped the ascent I saw the waters of the Sutlej shining like a silver bar below. Then Pornic blundered heavily on his nose, and we rolled together down some unseen slope.

I must have lost consciousness, for when I recovered I was lying on my stomach in a heap of soft white sand, and the dawn was beginning to break dimly over the edge of the slope down

which I had fallen.   As the light grew stronger I
saw that I was at the bottom of a horseshoe-
shaped crater of sand, opening on one side directly on to the shoals of the Sutlej.   My fever
had altogether left me, and, with the exception
of a slight dizziness in the head, I felt no bad ef-
fects from the fall over night.

Pornic, who was standing a few yards away,
was naturally a good deal exhausted, but had not
hurt himself in the least.   His saddle, a favorite
polo one, was much knocked about, and had been
twisted under his belly.   It took me some time
to put him to rights, and in the meantime I had
ample opportunities of observing the spot into
which I had so foolishly dropped.

At the risk of being considered tedious, I must
describe it at length; inasmuch as an accurate
mental picture of its peculiarities will be of material assistance in enabling the reader to understand what follows.

Imagine then, as I have said before, a horse-
shoe-shaped crater of sand with steeply graded
sand walls about thirty-five feet high.   (The
slope, I fancy, must have been about 65°.)   This
crater enclosed a level piece of ground about fifty
yards long by thirty at its broadest part, with a
rude well in the centre.   Round the bottom of
the crater, about three feet from the level of the
ground proper, ran a series of eighty-three semi-

circular, ovoid, square, and multilateral holes, all
about three feet at the mouth. Each hole on in-
spection showed that it was carefully shored in-
ternally with drift-wood and bamboos, and over
the mouth a wooden drip-board projected, like
the peak of a jockey's cap, for two feet. No
sign of life was visible in these tunnels, but a
most sickening stench pervaded the entire amphitheatre—a stench fouler than any which my
wanderings in Indian villages have introduced
me to.

Having remounted Pornic, who was as anxious
as I to get back to camp, I rode round the base of
the horseshoe to find some place whence an exit
would be practicable. The inhabitants, whoever
they might be, had not thought fit to put in an
appearance, so I was left to my own devices.
My first attempt to "rush" Pornic up the steep
sand-banks showed me that I had fallen into a
trap exactly on the same model as that which the
ant-lion sets for its prey. At each step the shift-
ing sand poured down from above in tons, and
rattled on the drip-boards of the holes like small
shot. A couple of ineffectual charges sent us
both rolling down to the bottom, half choked
with the torrents of sand; and I was constrained
to turn my attention to the river-bank.

Here everything seemed easy enough. The
sand hills ran down to the river edge, it is true,

but there were plenty of shoals and shallows
across which I could gallop Pornic, and find my
way back to *terra firma* by turning sharply to
the right or the left. As I led Pornic over the
sands I was startled by the faint pop of a rifle
across the river; and at the same moment a bullet
dropped with a sharp "*whit*" close to Pornic's
head.

There was no mistaking the nature of the
missile—a regulation Martini-Henry "picket."
About five hundred yards away a country-boat
was anchored in midstream; and a jet of smoke
drifting away from its bows in the still morning
air showed me whence the delicate attention had
come. Was ever a respectable gentleman in
such an *impasse?* The treacherous sand slope
allowed no escape from a spot which I had
visited most involuntarily, and a promenade on
the river frontage was the signal for a bombard-
ment from some insane native in a boat. I'm
afraid that I lost my temper very much indeed.

Another bullet reminded me that I had better
save my breath to cool my porridge; and I retreated hastily up the sands and back to the
horseshoe, where I saw that the noise of the rifle
had drawn sixty-five human beings from the
badger-holes which I had up till that point supposed to be untenanted. I found myself in the
midst of a crowd of spectators—about forty men,

twenty women, and one child who could not have been more than five years old. They were all scantily clothed in that salmon-colored cloth which one associates with Hindu mendicants, and, at first sight, gave me the impression of a band of loathsome *fakirs*. The filth and repulsiveness of the assembly were beyond all description, and I shuddered to think what their life in the badger-holes must be.

Even in these days, when local self-government has destroyed the greater part of a native's respect for a Sahib, I have been accustomed to a certain amount of civility from my inferiors, and on approaching the crowd naturally expected that there would be some recognition of my presence. As a matter of fact there was; but it was by no means what I had looked for.

The ragged crew actually laughed at me—such laughter I hope I may never hear again. They cackled, yelled, whistled, and howled as I walked into their midst; some of them literally throwing themselves down on the ground in convulsions of unholy mirth. In a moment I had let go Pornic's head, and, irritated beyond expression at the morning's adventure, commenced cuffing those nearest to me with all the force I could. The wretches dropped under my blows like nine-pins, and the laughter gave place to wails for mercy; while those yet untouched clasped me round the knees, imploring me in all sorts of uncouth tongues to spare them.

In the tumult, and just when I was feeling very much ashamed of myself for having thus easily given way to my temper, a thin, high voice murmured in English from behind my shoulder:— "Sahib! Sahib! Do you not know me? Sahib, it is Gunga Dass, the telegraph-master."

I spun round quickly and faced the speaker.

Gunga Dass (I have, of course, no hesitation in mentioning the man's real name) I had known four years before as a Deccanee Brahmin loaned by the Punjab Government to one of the Khalsia States. He was in charge of a branch telegraph-office there, and when I had last met him was a jovial, full-stomached, portly Government servant with a marvelous capacity for making bad puns in English—a peculiarity which made me remember him long after I had forgotten his services to me in his official capacity. It is seldom that a Hindu makes English puns.

Now, however, the man was changed beyond all recognition. Caste-mark, stomach, slate-colored continuations, and unctuous speech were all gone. I looked at a withered skeleton, turbanless and almost naked, with long matted hair and deep-set codfish-eyes. But for a crescent-shaped scar on the left cheek—the result of an accident for which I was responsible—I should

never have known him.   But it was indubitably
Gunga Dass, and—for this I was thankful—an
English-speaking native who might at least tell
me the meaning of all that I had gone through
that day.

The crowd retreated to some distance as I
turned toward the miserable figure, and ordered
him to show me some method of escaping from
the crater.   He held a freshly plucked crow in
his hand, and in reply to my question climbed
slowly on a platform of sand which ran in front
of the holes, and commenced lighting a fire there
in silence.   Dried bents, sand-poppies, and drift-
wood burn quickly; and I derived much consolation from the fact that he lit them with an ordinary sulphur-match.   When they were in a bright
glow, and the crow was neatly spitted in front
thereof, Gunga Dass began without a word of
preamble:

"There are only two kinds of men, Sar.   The
alive and the dead.   When you are dead you are
dead, but when you are alive you live."   (Here
the crow demanded his attention for an instant
as it twirled before the fire in danger of being
burned to a cinder.)   "If you die at home and
do not die when you come to the ghât to be
burned you come here."

The nature of the reeking village was made
plain now, and all that I had known or read of

the grotesque and the horrible paled before the
fact just communicated by the ex-Brahmin. Six-
teen years ago, when I first landed in Bombay, I
had been told by a wandering Armenian of the
existence, somewhere in India, of a place to
which such Hindus as had the misfortune to recover from trance or catalepsy were conveyed
and kept, and I recollect laughing heartily at
what I was then pleased to consider a traveler's
tale. Sitting at the bottom of the sand-trap, the
memory of Watson's Hotel, with its swinging
punkahs, white-robed attendants, and the sal-
low-faced Armenian, rose up in my mind as viv-
idly as a photograph, and I burst into a loud fit
of laughter. The contrast was too absurd!

Gunga Dass, as he bent over the unclean bird,
watched me curiously. Hindus seldom laugh,
and his surroundings were not such as to move
Gunga Dass to any undue excess of hilarity. He
removed the crow solemnly from the wooden
spit and as solemnly devoured it. Then he continued his story, which I give in his own words:

"In epidemics of the cholera you are carried
to be burned almost before you are dead. When
you come to the riverside the cold air, perhaps,
makes you alive, and then, if you are only little
alive, mud is put on your nose and mouth and
you die conclusively. If you are rather more
alive, more mud is put; but if you are too lively

they let you go and take you away. I was too lively, and made protestation with anger against the indignities that they endeavored to press upon me. In those days I was Brahmin and proud man. Now I am dead man and eat"— here he eyed the well-gnawed breast bone with the first sign of emotion that I had seen in him since we met—"crows, and other things. They took me from my sheets when they saw that I was too lively and gave me medicines for one week, and I survived successfully. Then they sent me by rail from my place to Okara Station, with a man to take care of me; and at Okara Station we met two other men, and they conducted we three on camels, in the night, from Okara Station to this place, and they propelled me from the top to the bottom, and the other two succeeded, and I have been here ever since two and a half years. Once I was Brahmin and proud man, and now I eat crows."

"There is no way of getting out?"

"None of what kind at all. When I first came I made experiments frequently and all the others also, but we have always succumbed to the sand which is precipitated upon our heads."

"But surely," I broke in at this point, "the river-front is open, and it is worth while dodging the bullets; while at night"—

I had already matured a rough plan of escape

which a natural instinct of selfishness forbade me sharing with Gunga Dass. He, however, divined my unspoken thought almost as soon as it was formed; and, to my intense astonishment, gave vent to a long low chuckle of derision—the laughter, be it understood, of a superior or at least of an equal.

"You will not"—he had dropped the Sir completely after his opening sentence—"make any escape that way. But you can try. I have tried. Once only."

The sensation of nameless terror and abject fear which I had in vain attempted to strive against overmastered me completely. My long fast—it was now close upon ten o'clock, and I had eaten nothing since tiffin on the previous day—combined with the violent and unnatural agitation of the ride had exhausted me, and I verily believe that, for a few minutes, I acted as one mad. I hurled myself against the pitiless sand-slope. I ran round the base of the crater, blaspheming and praying by turns. I crawled out among the sedges of the river-front, only to be driven back each time in an agony of nervous dread by the rifle-bullets which cut up the sand round me—for I dared not face the death of a mad dog among that hideous crowd—and finally fell, spent and raving, at the curb of the well. No one had taken the slightest notice of an exhibition which makes me blush hotly even when I think of it now.

Two or three men trod on my panting body as they drew water, but they were evidently used to this sort of thing, and had no time to waste upon me. The situation was humiliating. Gunga Dass, indeed, when he had banked the embers of his fire with sand, was at some pains to throw half a cupful of fetid water over my head, an attention for which I could have fallen on my knees and thanked him, but he was laughing all the while in the same mirthless, wheezy key that greeted me on my first attempt to force the shoals. And so, in a semi-comatose condition, I lay till noon. Then, being only a man after all, I felt hungry, and intimated as much to Gunga Dass, whom I had begun to regard as my natural protector. Following the impulse of the outer world when dealing with natives, I put my hand into my pocket and drew out four annas. The absurdity of the gift struck me at once, and I was about to replace the money.

Gunga Dass, however, was of a different opinion. "Give me the money," said he; "all you have, or I will get help, and we will kill you!" All this as if it were the most natural thing in the world!

A Briton's first impulse, I believe, is to guard the contents of his pockets; but a moment's re-

flection convinced me of the futility of differing
with the one man who had it in his power to
make me comfortable; and with whose help it
was possible that I might eventually escape from
the crater. I gave him all the money in my
possession, Rs. 9-8-5—nine rupees eight annas
and five pie—for I always keep small change as
bakshish when I am in camp. Gunga Dass
clutched the coins, and hid them at once in his
ragged loin-cloth, his expression changing to
something diabolical as he looked round to assure
himself that no one had observed us.

"*Now* I will give you something to eat,"
said he.

What pleasure the possession of my money
could have afforded him I am unable to say; but
inasmuch as it did give him evident delight I
was not sorry that I had parted with it so readily,
for I had no doubt that he would have had me
killed if I had refused. One does not protest
against the vagaries of a den of wild beasts; and
my companions were lower than any beasts.
While I devoured what Gunga Dass had provided, a coarse *chapatti* and a cupful of the foul
well-water, the people showed not the faintest
sign of curiosity—that curiosity which is so
rampant, as a rule, in an Indian village.

I could even fancy that they despised me. At
all events they treated me with the most chilling

indifference, and Gunga Dass was nearly as bad.
I plied him with questions about the terrible
village, and received extremely unsatisfactory
answers. So far as I could gather, it had been in
existence from time immemorial—whence I concluded that it was at least a century old—and
during that time no one had ever been known to
escape from it. [I had to control myself here
with both hands, lest the blind terror should lay
hold of me a second time and drive me raving
round the crater.] Gunga Dass took a malicious
pleasure in emphasizing this point and in watching me wince. Nothing that I could do would
induce him to tell me who the mysterious
" They " were.

" It is so ordered," he would reply, " and I
do not yet know any one who has disobeyed the
orders."

" Only wait till my servants find that I am
missing," I retorted, "and I promise you that
this place shall be cleared off the face of the
earth, and I'll give you a lesson in civility, too,
my friend."

" Your servants would be torn in pieces
before they came near this place; and, besides,
you are dead, my dear friend. It is not your
fault, of course, but none the less you are dead
and buried."

At irregular intervals supplies of food, I was

told, were dropped down from the land side into the amphitheatre, and the inhabitants fought for them like wild beasts. When a man felt his death coming on he retreated to his lair and died there. The body was sometimes dragged out of the hole and thrown on to the sand, or allowed to rot where it lay.

The phrase "thrown on to the sand" caught my attention, and I asked Gunga Dass whether this sort of thing was not likely to breed a pestilence.

"That," said he, with another of his wheezy chuckles, "you may see for yourself subsequently. You will have much time to make observations."

Whereat, to his great delight, I winced once more and hastily continued the conversation:— "And how do you live here from day to day? What do you do?" The question elicited exactly the same answer as before—coupled with the information that "this place is like your European heaven; there is neither marrying nor giving in marriage."

Gunga Dass has been educated at a Mission School, and, as he himself admitted, had he only changed his religion "like a wise man," might have avoided the living grave which was now his portion. But as long as I was with him I fancy he was happy.

Here was a Sahib, a representative of the dominant race, helpless as a child and completely at the mercy of his native neighbors. In a deliberate lazy way he set himself to torture me as a schoolboy would devote a rapturous half-hour to watching the agonies of an impaled beetle, or as a ferret in a blind burrow might glue himself comfortably to the neck of a rabbit. The burden of his conversation was that there was no escape "of no kind whatever," and that I should stay here till I died and was "thrown on to the sand." If it were possible to forejudge the conversation of the Damned on the advent of a new soul in their abode, I should say that they would speak as Gunga Dass did to me throughout that long afternoon. I was powerless to protest or answer; all my energies being devoted to a struggle against the inexplicable terror that threatened to overwhelm me again and again. I can compare the feeling to nothing except the struggles of a man against the overpowering nausea of the Channel passage—only my agony was of the spirit and infinitely more terrible.

As the day wore on, the inhabitants began to appear in full strength to catch the rays of the afternoon sun, which were now sloping in at the mouth of the crater. They assembled in little knots, and talked among themselves without even throwing a glance in my direction. About

four o'clock, as far as I could judge, Gunga Dass
rose and dived into his lair for a moment,
emerging with a live crow in his hands. The
wretched bird was in a most draggled and
deplorable condition, but seemed to be in no way
afraid of its master. Advancing cautiously to the
river front, Gunga Dass stepped from tussock to
tussock until he had reached a smooth patch of
sand directly in the line of the boat's fire. The
occupants of the boat took no notice. Here he
stopped, and, with a couple of dexterous turns
of the wrist, pegged the bird on its back with
outstretched wings. As was only natural, the
crow began to shriek at once and beat the air
with its claws. In a few seconds the clamor had
attracted the attention of a bevy of wild crows
on a shoal a few hundred yards away, where
they were discussing something that looked like
a corpse. Half a dozen crows flew over at once
to see what was going on, and also, as it proved,
to attack the pinioned bird. Gunga Dass, who
had lain down on a tussock, motioned to me
to be quiet, though I fancy this was a need-
less precaution. In a moment, and before I
could see how it happened, a wild crow, who
had grappled with the shrieking and helpless
bird, was entangled in the latter's claws, swiftly
disengaged by Gunga Dass, and pegged down
beside its companion in adversity. Curiosity, it

seemed, overpowered the rest of the flock, and almost before Gunga Dass and I had time to withdraw to the tussock, two more captives were struggling in the upturned claws of the decoys. So the chase—if I can give it so dignified a name—continued until Gunga Dass had captured seven crows. Five of them he throttled at once, reserving two for further operations another day. I was a good deal impressed by this, to me, novel method of securing food, and complimented Gunga Dass on his skill.

"It is nothing to do," said he. "To-morrow you must do it for me. You are stronger than I am."

This calm assumption of superiority upset me not a little, and I answered peremptorily;—"Indeed, you old ruffian! What do you think I have given you money for?"

"Very well," was the unmoved reply. "Perhaps not to-morrow, nor the day after, nor subsequently; but in the end, and for many years, you will catch crows and eat crows, and you will thank your European God that you have crows to catch and eat."

I could have cheerfully strangled him for this; but judged it best under the circumstances to smother my resentment. An hour later I was eating one of the crows; and, as Gunga Dass had said, thanking my God that I had a crow to

eat. Never as long as I live shall I forget that
evening meal. The whole population were
squatting on the hard sand platform opposite
their dens, huddled over tiny fires of refuse and
dried rushes. Death, having once laid his hand
upon these men and forborne to strike, seemed
to stand aloof from them now; for most of our
company were old men, bent and worn and
twisted with years, and women aged to all appearance as the Fates themselves. They sat together in knots and talked—God only knows
what they found to discuss—in low equable
tones, curiously in contrast to the strident babble
with which natives are accustomed to make day
hideous. Now and then an access of that sudden
fury which had possessed me in the morning
would lay hold on a man or woman; and with
yells and imprecations the sufferer would attack
the steep slope until, baffled and bleeding, he fell
back on the platform incapable of moving a
limb. The others would never even raise their
eyes when this happened, as men too well aware
of the futility of their fellows' attempts and
wearied with their useless repetition. I saw four
such outbursts in the course of that evening.

Gunga Dass took an eminently business-like
view of my situation, and while we were dining
—I can afford to laugh at the recollection now,
but it was painful enough at the time—pro-

pounded the terms on which he would consent
to "do" for me. My nine rupees eight annas,
he argued, at the rate of three annas a day, would
provide me with food for fifty-one days, or about
seven weeks; that is to say, he would be willing
to cater for me for that length of time. At the
end of it I was to look after myself. For a further consideration—*videlicet* my boots—he would
be willing to allow me to occupy the den next
to his own, and would supply me with as much
dried grass for bedding as he could spare.

"Very well, Gunga Dass," I replied; "to the
first terms I cheerfully agree, but, as there is
nothing on earth to prevent my killing you as you
sit here and taking everything that you have" (I
thought of the two invaluable crows at the time),
"I flatly refuse to give you my boots and shall
take whichever den I please."

The stroke was a bold one, and I was glad
when I saw that it had succeeded. Gunga Dass
changed his tone immediately, and disavowed
all intention of asking for my boots. At the
time it did not strike me as at all strange that I, a
Civil Engineer, a man of thirteen years' standing
in the Service, and, I trust, an average Englishman, should thus calmly threaten murder and
violence against the man who had, for a consideration it is true, taken me under his wing. I
had left the world, it seemed, for centuries. I

was as certain then as I am now of my own existence, that in the accursed settlement there was no law save that of the strongest; that the living dead men had thrown behind them every canon of the world which had cast them out; and that I had to depend for my own life on my strength and vigilance alone. The crew of the ill-fated Mignonette are the only men who would understand my frame of mind. "At present," I argued to myself, "I am strong and a match for six of these wretches. It is imperatively necessary that I should, for my own sake, keep both health and strength until the hour of my release comes—if it ever does."

Fortified with these resolutions, I ate and drank as much as I could, and made Gunga Dass understand that I intended to be his master, and that the least sign of insubordination on his part would be visited with the only punishment I had it in my power to inflict—sudden and violent death. Shortly after this I went to bed. That is to say, Gunga Dass gave me a double armful of dried bents which I thrust down the mouth of the lair to the right of his, and followed myself, feet foremost; the hole running about nine feet into the sand with a slight downward inclination, and being neatly shored with timbers. From my den, which faced the river-front, I was able to watch the waters of the Sutlej flowing past under

the light of a young moon and compose myself
to sleep as best I might.

The horrors of that night I shall never forget.
My den was nearly as narrow as a coffin, and the
sides had been worn smooth and greasy by the
contact of innumerable naked bodies, added to
which it smelled abominably. Sleep was altogether out of question to one in my excited frame
of mind. As the night wore on, it seemed that
the entire amphitheatre was filled with legions of
unclean devils that, trooping up from the shoals
below, mocked the unfortunates in their lairs.

Personally I am not of an imaginative tempera-
ment,—very few Engineers are,—but on that
occasion I was as completely prostrated with
nervous terror as any woman. After half an
hour or so, however, I was able once more to
calmly review my chances of escape. Any exit
by the steep sand walls was, of course, impracti-
cable. I had been thoroughly convinced of this
some time before. It was possible, just possible,
that I might, in the uncertain moonlight, safely
run the gauntlet of the rifle shots. The place
was so full of terror for me that I was prepared
to undergo any risk in leaving it. Imagine my
delight, then, when after creeping stealthily to
the river-front I found that the infernal boat was
not there. My freedom lay before me in the
next few steps!

By walking out to the first shallow pool that lay at the foot of the projecting left horn of the horseshoe, I could wade across, turn the flank of the crater, and make my way inland. Without a moment's hesitation I marched briskly past the tussocks where Gunga Dass had snared the crows, and out in the direction of the smooth white sand beyond. My first step from the tufts of dried grass showed me how utterly futile was any hope of escape; for, as I put my foot down, I felt an indescribable drawing, sucking motion of the sand below. Another moment and my leg was swallowed up nearly to the knee. In the moonlight the whole surface of the sand seemed to be shaken with devilish delight at my disappointment. I struggled clear, sweating with terror and exertion, back to the tussocks behind me and fell on my face.

My only means of escape from the semicircle was protected with a quicksand!

How long I lay I have not the faintest idea; but I was roused at last by the malevolent chuckle of Gunga Dass at my ear. "I would advise you, Protector of the Poor" (the ruffian was speaking English) "to return to your house. It is unhealthy to lie down here. Moreover, when the boat returns, you will most certainly be rifled at." He stood over me in the dim light of the dawn, chuckling and laughing to himself.

Suppressing my first impulse to catch the man by the neck and throw him on to the quicksand, I rose sullenly and followed him to the platform below the burrows.

Suddenly, and futilely as I thought while I spoke, I asked:—"Gunga Dass, what is the good of the boat if I can't get out *anyhow?*" I recollect that even in my deepest trouble I had been speculating vaguely on the waste of ammunition in guarding an already well protected foreshore.

Gunga Dass laughed again and made answer: —"They have the boat only in daytime. It is for the reason that *there is a way*. I hope we shall have the pleasure of your company for much longer time. It is a pleasant spot when you have been here some years and eaten roast crow long enough."

I staggered, numbed and helpless, toward the fetid burrow allotted to me, and fell asleep. An hour or so later I was awakened by a piercing scream—the shrill, high-pitched scream of a horse in pain. Those who have once heard that will never forget the sound. I found some little difficulty in scrambling out of the burrow. When I was in the open, I saw Pornic, my poor old Pornic, lying dead on the sandy soil. How they had killed him I cannot guess. Gunga Dass explained that horse was better than crow, and "greatest good of greatest number is political maxim. We are now Republic, Mister Jukes, and you are entitled to a fair share of the beast. If you like, we will pass a vote of thanks. Shall I propose?"

Yes, we were a Republic indeed! A Republic of wild beasts penned at the bottom of a pit, to eat and fight and sleep till we died. I attempted no protest of any kind, but sat down and stared at the hideous sight in front of me. In less time almost than it takes me to write this, Pornic's body was divided, in some unclean way or other; the men and women had dragged the fragments on to the platform and were preparing their morning meal. Gunga Dass cooked mine. The almost irresistible impulse to fly at the sand walls until I was wearied laid hold of me afresh, and I had to struggle against it with all my might. Gunga Dass was offensively jocular till I told him that if he addressed another remark of any kind whatever to me I should strangle him where he sat. This silenced him till silence became insupportable, and I bade him say something.

"You will live here till you die like the other Feringhi," he said, coolly, watching me over the fragment of gristle that he was gnawing.

"What other Sahib, you swine? Speak at once, and don't stop to tell me a lie."

"He is over there," answered Gunga Dass, pointing to a burrow-mouth about four doors to

the left of my own. "You can see for yourself.
He died in the burrow as you will die, and I will
die, and as all these men and women and the one
child will also die."

"For pity's sake tell me all you know about
him. Who was he? When did he come, and
when did he die?"

This appeal was a weak step on my part.
Gunga Dass only leered and replied:—"I will
not—unless you give me something first."

Then I recollected where I was, and struck the
man between the eyes, partially stunning him.
He stepped down from the platform at once,
and, cringing and fawning and weeping and attempting to embrace my feet, led me round to
the burrow which he had indicated.

"I know nothing whatever about the gentleman. Your God be my witness that I do not.
He was as anxious to escape as you were, and
he was shot from the boat, though we all did all
things to prevent him from attempting. He was
shot here." Gunga Dass laid his hand on his lean
stomach and bowed to the earth.

"Well, and what then? Go on!"

"And then—and then, Your Honor, we carried
him in to his house and gave him water, and put
wet cloths on the wound, and he laid down in
his house and gave up the ghost."

"In how long? In how long?"

"About half an hour, after he received his wound. I call Vishn to witness," yelled the wretched man, "that I did everything for him. Everything which was possible, that I did!"

He threw himself down on the ground and clasped my ankles. But I had my doubts about Gunga Dass's benevolence, and kicked him off as he lay protesting.

"I believe you robbed him of everything he had. But I can find out in a minute or two. How long was the Sahib here?"

"Nearly a year and a half. I think he must have gone mad. But hear me swear, Protector of the Poor! Won't Your Honor hear me swear that I never touched an article that belonged to him? What is Your Worship going to do?"

I had taken Gunga Dass by the waist and had hauled him on to the platform opposite the deserted burrow. As I did so I thought of my wretched fellow-prisoner's unspeakable misery among all these horrors for eighteen months, and the final agony of dying like a rat in a hole, with a bullet-wound in the stomach. Gunga Dass fancied I was going to kill him and howled pitifully. The rest of the population, in the plethora that follows a full flesh meal, watched us without stirring.

"Go inside, Gunga Dass," said I, "and fetch it out."

I was feeling sick and faint with horror now. Gunga Dass nearly rolled off the platform and howled aloud.

"But I am Brahmin, Sahib—a high-caste Brahmin. By your soul, by your father's soul, do not make me do this thing!"

"Brahmin or no Brahmin, by my soul and my father's soul, in you go!" I said, and, seizing him by the shoulders, I crammed his head into the mouth of the burrow, kicked the rest of him in, and, sitting down, covered my face with my hands.

At the end of a few minutes I heard a rustle and a creak; then Gunga Dass in a sobbing, choking whisper speaking to himself; then a soft thud—and I uncovered my eyes.

The dry sand had turned the corpse entrusted to its keeping into a yellow-brown mummy. I told Gunga Dass to stand off while I examined it. The body—clad in an olive-green hunting-suit much stained and worn, with leather pads on the shoulders—was that of a man between thirty and forty, above middle height, with light, sandy hair, long mustache, and a rough unkempt beard. The left canine of the upper jaw was missing, and a portion of the lobe of the right ear was gone. On the second finger of the left hand was a ring—a shield-shaped bloodstone set in gold, with a monogram that might have been either

"B.K." or "B.L." On the third finger of the right hand was a silver ring in the shape of a coiled cobra, much worn and tarnished. Gunga Dass deposited a handful of trifles he had picked out of the burrow at my feet, and, covering the face of the body with my handkerchief, I turned to examine these. I give the full list in the hope that it may lead to the identification of the unfortunate man:

1. Bowl of a briarwood pipe, serrated at the edge; much worn and blackened; bound with string at the screw.

2. Two patent-lever keys; wards of both broken.

3. Tortoise-shell-handled penknife, silver or nickel, name-plate, marked with monogram "B.K."

4. Envelope, postmark undecipherable, bearing a Victorian stamp, addressed to "Miss Mon—" (rest illegible)—"ham"—"nt."

5. Imitation crocodile-skin notebook with pencil. First forty-five pages blank; four and a-half illegible; fifteen others filled with private memoranda relating chiefly to three persons—a Mrs. L. Singleton, abbreviated several times to "Lot Single," "Mrs. S. May," and "Garmison," referred to in places as "Jerry" or "Jack."

6. Handle of small-sized hunting-knife.

Blade snapped short. Buck's horn, diamond cut, with swivel and ring on the butt; fragment of cotton cord attached.

It must not be supposed that I inventoried all these things on the spot as fully as I have here written them down. The notebook first attracted my attention, and I put it in my pocket with a view to studying it later on. The rest of the articles I conveyed to my burrow for safety's sake, and there, being a methodical man, I inventoried them. I then returned to the corpse and ordered Gunga Dass to help me to carry it out to the river-front. While we were engaged in this, the exploded shell of an old brown cartridge dropped out of one of the pockets and rolled at my feet. Gunga Dass had not seen it; and I fell to thinking that a man does not carry exploded cartridge-cases, especially "browns," which will not bear loading twice, about with him when shooting. In other words, that cartridge-case has been fired inside the crater. Consequently there must be a gun somewhere. I was on the verge of asking Gunga Dass, but checked myself, knowing that he would lie. We laid the body down on the edge of the quicksand by the tussocks. It was my intention to push it out and let it be swallowed up—the only possible mode of burial that I could think of. I ordered Gunga Dass to go away.

Then I gingerly put the corpse out on the quicksand. In doing so, it was lying face downward, I tore the frail and rotten khaki shooting-coat open, disclosing a hideous cavity in the back. I have already told you that the dry sand had, as it were, mummified the body. A moment's glance showed that the gaping hole had been caused by a gun-shot wound; the gun must have been fired with the muzzle almost touching the back. The shooting-coat, being intact, had been drawn over the body after death, which must have been instantaneous. The secret of the poor wretch's death was plain to me in a flash. Some one of the crater, presumably Gunga Dass, must have shot him with his own gun—the gun that fitted the brown cartridges. He had never attempted to escape in the face of the rifle-fire from the boat.

I pushed the corpse out hastily, and saw it sink from sight literally in a few seconds. I shuddered as I watched. In a dazed, half-conscious way I turned to peruse the notebook. A stained and discolored slip of paper had been inserted between the binding and the back, and dropped out as I opened the pages. This is what it contained:—"*Four out from crow-clump: three left; nine out; two right; three back; two left; fourteen out; two left; seven out; one left; nine back; two right; six back;*

four right; seven back." The paper had been burned and charred at the edges. What it meant I could not understand. I sat down on the dried bents turning it over and over between my fingers, until I was aware of Gunga Dass standing immediately behind me with glowing eyes and outstretched hands.

"Have you got it?" he panted. "Will you not let me look at it also? I swear that I will return it."

"Got what? Return what?" I asked.

"That which you have in your hands. It will help us both." He stretched out his long, bird-like talons, trembling with eagerness.

"I could never find it," he continued. "He had secreted it about his person. Therefore I shot him, but nevertheless I was unable to obtain it."

Gunga Dass had quite forgotten his little fiction about the rifle-bullet. I received the information perfectly calmly. Morality is blunted by consorting with the Dead who are alive.

"What on earth are you raving about? What is it you want me to give you?"

"The piece of paper in the notebook. It will help us both. Oh, you fool! You fool! Can you not see what it will do for us? We shall escape!"

His voice rose almost to a scream, and he

danced with excitement before me. I own I was moved at the chance of getting away.

"Don't skip! Explain yourself. Do you mean to say that this slip of paper will help us? What does it mean?"

"Read it aloud! Read it aloud! I beg and I pray you to read it aloud."

I did so. Gunga Dass listened delightedly, and drew an irregular line in the sand with his fingers.

"See now! It was the length of his gun-barrels without the stock. I have those barrels. Four gun-barrels out from the place where I caught crows. Straight out; do you follow me? Then three left— Ah! how well I remember when that man worked it out night after night. Then nine out, and so on. Out is always straight before you across the quicksand. He told me so before I killed him."

"But if you knew all this why didn't you get out before?"

"I did *not* know it. He told me that he was working it out a year and a half ago, and how he was working it out night after night when the boat had gone away, and he could get out near the quicksand safely. Then he said that we would get away together. But I was afraid that he would leave me behind one night when ne had worked it all out, and so I shot him. Besides, it is not advisable that the men who once get in here should escape. Only I, and *I* am a Brahmin."

The prospect of escape had brought Gunga Dass's caste back to him. He stood up, walked about and gesticulated violently. Eventually I managed to make him talk soberly, and he told me how this Englishman had spent six months night after night in exploring, inch by inch, the passage across the quicksand; how he had declared it to be simplicity itself up to within about twenty yards of the river bank after turning the flank of the left horn of the horseshoe. This much he had evidently not completed when Gunga Dass shot him with his own gun.

In my frenzy of delight at the possibilities of escape I recollect shaking hands effusively with Gunga Dass, after we had decided that we were to make an attempt to get away that very night. It was weary work waiting throughout the afternoon.

About ten o'clock, as far as I could judge, when the Moon had just risen above the lip of the crater, Gunga Dass made a move for his burrow to bring out the gun-barrels whereby to measure our path. All the other wretched inhabitants had retired to their lairs long ago. The guardian boat drifted down-stream some hours before, and we were utterly alone by the crow-clump. Gunga Dass, while carrying the gun-barrels, let slip the piece of paper which was to be our guide. I stooped down hastily to recover it, and, as I did so, I was aware that the diabolical Brahmin was aiming a violent blow at the back of my head with the gun-barrels. It was too late to turn round. I must have received the blow somewhere on the nape of my neck. A hundred thousand fiery stars danced before my eyes, and I fell forward senseless at the edge of the quicksand.

When I recovered consciousness, the Moon was going down, and I was sensible of intolerable pain in the back of my head. Gunga Dass had disappeared and my mouth was full of blood. I lay down again and prayed that I might die without more ado. Then the unreasoning fury which I have before mentioned laid hold upon me, and I staggered inland toward the walls of the crater. It seemed that some one was calling to me in a whisper—"Sahib! Sahib! Sahib!" exactly as my bearer used to call me in the mornings. I fancied that I was delirious until a handful of sand fell at my feet. Then I looked up and saw a head peering down into the amphitheatre—the head of Dunnoo, my dog-boy, who attended to my collies. As soon as he had attracted my attention, he held up his hand and showed a rope. I motioned, staggering to and fro the while, that he should throw it down. It was a couple of leather punkah-ropes knotted together, with a loop at one end. I slipped the loop over my head and under my arms; heard Dunnoo urge something forward; was conscious that I was being dragged, face downward, up the steep sand slope, and the next instant found myself choked and half fainting on the sand hills overlooking the crater. Dunnoo, with his face ashy grey in the moonlight, implored me not to stay but to get back to my tent at once.

It seems that he had tracked Pornic's footprints fourteen miles across the sands to the crater; had returned and told my servants, who flatly refused to meddle with any one, white or black, once fallen into the hideous Village of the Dead; whereupon Dunnoo had taken one of my ponies and a couple of pukah-ropes, returned to the crater, and hauled me out as I have described.

To cut a long story short, Dunnoo is now my personal servant on a gold mohur a month—a sum which I still think far too little for the services he has rendered. Nothing on earth will induce me to go near that devilish spot again, or to reveal its whereabouts more clearly than I have done. Of Gunga Dass I have never found a trace, nor do I wish to do. My sole motive in giving this to be published is the hope that some one may possibly identify, from the details and the inventory which I have given above, the corpse of the man in the olive-green hunting-suit.

THE MAN WHO WOULD BE KING

THE MAN WHO WOULD BE KING

"Brother to a Prince and fellow to a beggar if he be found worthy."

THE Law, as quoted, lays down a fair conduct of life, and one not easy to follow. I have been fellow to a beggar again and again under circumstances which prevented either of us finding out whether the other was worthy. I have still to be brother to a Prince, though I once came near to kinship with what might have been a veritable King and was promised the reversion of a Kingdom—army, law-courts, revenue and policy all complete. But, to-day, I greatly fear that my King is dead, and if I want a crown I must go and hunt it for myself.

The beginning of everything was in a railway train upon the road to Mhow from Ajmir. There had been a Deficit in the Budget, which necessitated traveling, not Second-class, which is only half as dear as First-class, but by Intermediate, which is very awful indeed. There are no cushions in the Intermediate class, and the population are either Intermediate, which is Eurasian, or native, which for a long night journey is nasty, or Loafer, which is amusing though intoxicated.

Intermediates do not patronize refreshment-rooms. They carry their food in bundles and pots, and buy sweets from the native sweetmeat-sellers, and drink the roadside water. That is why in the hot weather Intermediates are taken out of the carriages dead, and in all weathers are most properly looked down upon.

My particular Intermediate happened to be empty till I reached Nasirabad, when a huge gentleman in shirt-sleeves entered, and, following the custom of Intermediates, passed the time cf day. He was a wanderer and a vagabond like myself, but with an educated taste for whiskey. He told tales of things he had seen and done, of out-of-the-way corners of the Empire into which he had penetrated, and of adventures in which he risked his life for a few days' food. "If India was filled with men like you and me, not knowing more than the crows where they'd get their next day's rations, it isn't seventy millions of revenue the land would be paying—it's seven hundred millions," said he; and as I looked at his mouth and chin I was disposed to agree with him. We talked politics—the politics of Loafer-dom that sees things from the underside where the lath and plaster is not smoothed off—and we talked postal arrangements because my friend wanted to send a telegram back from the next station to Ajmir, which is the turning-off place from the Bombay to the Mhow line as you travel westward. My friend had no money beyond eight annas which he wanted for dinner, and I had no money at all, owing to the hitch in the Budget before mentioned. Further, I was going into a wilderness where, though I should resume touch with the Treasury, there were no telegraph offices. I was, therefore, unable to help him in any way.

"We might threaten a Station-master, and make him send a wire on tick," said my friend, "but that'd mean inquiries for you and for me, and I've got my hands full these days. Did you say you are traveling back along this line within any days?"

"Within ten," I said.

"Can't you make it eight?" said he. "Mine is rather urgent business."

"I can send your telegram within ten days if that will serve you," I said.

"I couldn't trust the wire to fetch him now I think of it. It's this way. He leaves Delhi on the 23d for Bombay. That means he'll be running through Ajmir about the night of the 23d."

"But I'm going into the Indian Desert," I explained.

"Well *and* good," said he. "You'll be changing at Marwar Junction to get into Jodhpore territory—you must do that—and he'll be coming through Marwar Junction in the early morning of the 24th by the Bombay Mail. Can you be at Marwar Junction on that time? 'Twon't be inconveniencing you because I know that there's precious few pickings to be got out of these Central India States—even though you pretend to be correspondent of the *Backwoodsman*."

"Have you ever tried that trick?" I asked.

"Again and again, but the Residents find you out, and then you get escorted to the Border before you've time to get your knife into them. But about my friend here. I *must* give him a word o' mouth to tell him what's come to me or else he won't know where to go. I would take it more than kind of you if you was to come out of Central India in time to catch him at Marwar Junction, and say to him:—'He has gone South for the week.' He'll know what that means. He's a big man with a red beard, and a great swell he is. You'll find him sleeping like a gentleman with all his luggage round him in a Second-class compartment. But don't you be afraid. Slip down the window, and say:—'He has gone South for the week,' and he'll tumble. It's only cutting your time of stay in those parts by two days. I ask you as a stranger—going to the West," he said, with emphasis.

"Where have *you* come from?" said I.

"From the East," said he, "and I am hoping

that you will give him the message on the Square
—for the sake of my Mother as well as your
own."

Englishmen are not usually softened by appeals to the memory of their mothers, but for
certain reasons, which will be fully apparent, I
saw fit to agree.

"It's more than a little matter," said he, "and
that's why I ask you to do it—and now I know
that I can depend on you doing it. A Second-
class carriage at Marwar Junction, and a red-
haired man asleep in it. You'll be sure to remember. I get out at the next station, and I
must hold on there till he comes or sends me
what I want."

"I'll give the message if I catch him," I said,
"and for the sake of your Mother as well as
mine I'll give you a word of advice. Don't try
to run the Central India States just now as the
correspondent of the *Backwoodsman*. There's a
real one knocking about here, and it might lead
to trouble."

"Thank you," said he, simply, "and when will
the swine be gone? I can't starve because he's
ruining my work. I wanted to get hold of the
Degumber Rajah down here about his father's
widow, and give him a jump."

"What did he do to his father's widow,
then?"

"Filled her up with red pepper and slippered her to death as she hung from a beam. I found that out myself and I'm the only man that would dare going into the State to get hush-money for it. They'll try to poison me, same as they did in Chortumna when I went on the loot there. But you'll give the man at Marwar Junction my message?"

He got out at a little roadside station, and I reflected. I had heard, more than once, of men personating correspondents of newspapers and bleeding small Native States with threats of exposure, but I had never met any of the caste before. They lead a hard life, and generally die with great suddenness. The Native States have a wholesome horror of English newspapers, which may throw light on their peculiar methods of government, and do their best to choke correspondents with champagne, or drive them out of their mind with four-in-hand barouches. They do not understand that nobody cares a straw for the internal administration of Native States so long as oppression and crime are kept within decent limits, and the ruler is not drugged, drunk, or diseased from one end of the year to the other. Native States were created by Providence in order to supply picturesque scenery, tigers, and tall-writing. They are the dark places of the earth, full of unimaginable cruelty, touch-

ing the Railway and the Telegraph on one side,
and, on the other, the days of Harun-al-Raschid.
When I left the train I did business with divers
Kings, and in eight days passed through many
changes of life.   Sometimes I wore dress-clothes
and consorted with Princes and Politicals, drinking
from crystal and eating from silver.   Sometimes
I lay out upon the ground and devoured what I
could get, from a plate made of a flapjack, and
drank the running water, and slept under the
same rug as my servant.   It was all in the day's
work.

Then I headed for the Great Indian Desert upon
the proper date, as I had promised, and the night
Mail set me down at Marwar Junction, where a
funny little, happy-go-lucky, native-managed
railway runs to Jodhpore.   The Bombay Mail
from Delhi makes a short halt at Marwar.   She
arrived as I got in, and I had just time to hurry
to her platform and go down the carriages.
There was only one Second-class on the train.   I
slipped the window and looked down upon a
flaming red beard, half covered by a railway rug.
That was my man, fast asleep, and I dug him
gently in the ribs.   He woke with a grunt and I
saw his face in the light of the lamps.   It was a
great and shining face.

"Tickets again?" said he.

"No," said I.   "I am to tell you that he is

gone South for the week.   He is gone South for
the week!"

The train had begun to move out.   The red
man rubbed his eyes.   "He has gone South for
the week," he repeated.   "Now that's just like
his impidence.   Did he say that I was to give
you anything?—'Cause I won't."

"He didn't," I said, and dropped away, and
watched the red lights die out in the dark.   It
was horribly cold because the wind was blowing
off the sands.   I climbed into my own train—not
an Intermediate Carriage this time—and went to
sleep.

If the man with the beard had given me a
rupee I should have kept it as a memento of a
rather curious affair.   But the consciousness of
having done my duty was my only reward.

Later on I reflected that two gentlemen like my
friends could not do any good if they foregath-
ered and personated correspondents of newspapers, and might, if they "stuck up" one of
the little rat-trap states of Central India or South-
ern Rajputana, get themselves into serious diffi-
culties.   I therefore took some trouble to describe them as accurately as I could remember
to people who would be interested in deporting
them: and succeeded, so I was later informed,
in having them headed back from the Degumber
borders.

Then I became respectable, and returned to an Office where there were no Kings and no incidents except the daily manufacture of a newspaper. A newspaper office seems to attract every conceivable sort of person, to the prejudice of discipline. Zenana-mission ladies arrive, and beg that the Editor will instantly abandon all his duties to describe a Christian prize-giving in a back-slum of a perfectly inaccessible village; Colonels who have been overpassed for commands sit down and sketch the outline of a series of ten, twelve, or twenty-four leading articles on Seniority *versus* Selection; missionaries wish to know why they have not been permitted to escape from their regular vehicles of abuse and swear at a brother-missionary under special patronage of the editorial We; stranded theatrical companies troop up to explain that they cannot pay for their advertisements, but on their return from New Zealand or Tahiti will do so with interest; inventors of patent punkah-pulling machines, carriage couplings and unbreakable swords and axle-trees call with specifications in their pockets and hours at their disposal; tea-companies enter and elaborate their prospectuses with the office pens; secretaries of ball-committees clamor to have the glories of their last dance more fully expounded; strange ladies rustle in and say:—"I want a hundred lady's cards printed

at once, please," which is manifestly part of an
Editor's duty; and every dissolute ruffian that
ever tramped the Grand Trunk Road makes it his
business to ask for employment as a proof-
reader. And, all the time, the telephone-bell is
ringing madly, and Kings are being killed on the
Continent, and Empires are saying—" You're another," and Mister Gladstone is calling down
brimstone upon the British Dominions, and the
little black copy-boys are whining, " *kaa-pi chay-
ha-yek* " (copy wanted) like tired bees, and most
of the paper is as blank as Modred's shield.

But that is the amusing part of the year.
There are other six months wherein none ever
come to call, and the thermometer walks inch by
inch up to the top of the glass, and the office is
darkened to just above reading-light, and the
press machines are red-hot of touch, and nobody
writes anything but accounts of amusements in
the Hill-stations or obituary notices. Then the
telephone becomes a tinkling terror, because it
tells you of the sudden deaths of men and
women that you knew intimately, and the
prickly-heat covers you as with a garment, and
you sit down and write:—"A slight increase of
sickness is reported from the Khuda Janta Khan
District. The outbreak is purely sporadic in its
nature, and, thanks to the energetic efforts of the
District authorities, is now almost at an end. It

is, however, with deep regret we record the death, etc."

Then the sickness really breaks out, and the less recording and reporting the better for the peace of the subscribers. But the Empires and the Kings continue to divert themselves as selfishly as before, and the Foreman thinks that a daily paper really ought to come out once in twenty-four hours, and all the people at the Hill-stations in the middle of their amusements say:—"Good gracious! Why can't the paper be sparkling? I'm sure there's plenty going on up here."

That is the dark half of the moon, and, as the advertisements say, "must be experienced to be appreciated."

It was in that season, and a remarkably evil season, that the paper began running the last issue of the week on Saturday night, which is to say Sunday morning, after the custom of a London paper. This was a great convenience, for immediately after the paper was put to bed, the dawn would lower the thermometer from 96° to almost 84° for half an hour, and in that chill—you have no idea how cold is 84° on the grass until you begin to pray for it—a very tired man could set off to sleep ere the heat roused him.

One Saturday night it was my pleasant duty to

put the paper to bed alone.   A King or courtier
or a courtesan or a community was going to die
or get a new Constitution, or do something that
was important on the other side of the world,
and the paper was to be held open till the latest
possible minute in order to catch the telegram.
It was a pitchy black night, as stifling as a June
night can be, and the *loo*, the red-hot wind from
the westward, was booming among the tinder-
dry trees and pretending that the rain was on its
heels.   Now and again a spot of almost boiling
water would fall on the dust with the flop of a
frog, but all our weary world knew that was
only pretence.   It was a shade cooler in the
press-room than the office, so I sat there, while
the type ticked and clicked, and the night-jars
hooted at the windows, and the all but naked
compositors wiped the sweat from their foreheads and called for water.   The thing that was
keeping us back, whatever it was, would not
come off, though the *loo* dropped and the last
type was set, and the whole round earth stood
still in the choking heat, with its finger on its
lip, to wait the event.   I drowsed, and wondered
whether the telegraph was a blessing, and
whether this dying man, or struggling people,
was aware of the inconvenience the delay was
causing.   There was no special reason beyond
the heat and worry to make tension, but, as the

clock hands crept up to three o'clock and the machines spun their fly-wheels two and three times to see that all was in order, before I said the word that would set them off, I could have shrieked aloud.

Then the roar and rattle of the wheels shivered the quiet into little bits. I rose to go away, but two men in white clothes stood in front of me. The first one said:—"It's him!" The second said:—"So it is!" And they both laughed almost as loudly as the machinery roared, and mopped their foreheads. "We see there was a light burning across the road and we were sleeping in that ditch there for coolness, and I said to my friend here, The office is open. Let's come along and speak to him as turned us back from the Degumber State," said the smaller of the two. He was the man I had met in the Mhow train, and his fellow was the red-bearded man of Marwar Junction. There was no mistaking the eyebrows of the one or the beard of the other.

I was not pleased, because I wished to go to sleep, not to squabble with loafers. "What do you want?" I asked.

"Half an hour's talk with you cool and comfortable, in the office," said the red-bearded man. "We'd *like* some drink—the Contrack doesn't begin yet, Peachey, so you needn't look—but what we really want is advice. We don't want money. We ask you as a favor, because you did us a bad turn about Degumber."

I led from the press-room to the stifling office with the maps on the walls, and the red-haired man rubbed his hands. "That's something like," said he. "This was the proper shop to come to. Now, Sir, let me introduce to you Brother Peachey Carnehan, that's him, and Brother Daniel Dravot, that is *me*, and the less said about our professions the better, for we have been most things in our time. Soldier, sailo , compositor, photographer, proof-reader, street-preacher, and correspondents of the *Backwoodsman* when we thought the paper wanted one. Carnehan is sober, and so am I. Look at ɩ s first and see that's sure. It will save you cuttir ɡ into my talk. We'll take one of your cigars apiece, and you shall see us light."

I watched the test. The men were absolutely sober, so I gave them each a tepid peg.

"Well *and* good," said Carnehan of the eye-brows, wiping the froth from his moustache. "Let me talk now, Dan. We have been all over India, mostly on foot. We have been boiler-fitters, engine-drivers, petty contractors, and all that, and we have decided that India isn't big enough for such as us."

They certainly were too big for the office.

Dravot's beard seemed to fill half the room and Carnehan's shoulders the other half, as they sat on the big table. Carnehan continued:—
"The country isn't half worked out because they that governs it won't let you touch it. They spend all their blessed time in governing it, and you can't lift a spade, nor chip a rock, nor look for oil, nor anything like that without all the Government saying—'Leave it alone and let us govern.' Therefore, such as it is, we will let it alone, and go away to some other place where a man isn't crowded and can come to his own. We are not little men, and there is nothing that we are afraid of except Drink, and we have signed a Contrack on that. *Therefore*, we are going away to be Kings."

"Kings in our own right," muttered Dravot.

"Yes, of course," I said. "You've been tramping in the sun, and it's a very warm night, and hadn't you better sleep over the notion? Come to-morrow."

"Neither drunk nor sunstruck," said Dravot. "We have slept over the notion half a year, and require to see Books and Atlases, and we have decided that there is only one place now in the world that two strong men can Sar-a-*whack*. They call it Kafiristan. By my reckoning it's the top right-hand corner of Afghanistan, not more than three hundred miles from Peshawur. They have two and thirty heathen idols there, and we'll be the thirty-third. It's a mountaineous country, and the women of those parts are very beautiful."

"But that is provided against in the Contrack," said Carnehan. "Neither Women nor Liqu-or, Daniel."

"And that's all we know, except that no one has gone there, and they fight, and in any place where they fight a man who knows how to drill men can always be a King. We shall go to those parts and say to any King we find—'D' you want to vanquish your foes?' and we will show him how to drill men; for that we know better than anything else. Then we will subvert that King and seize his Throne and establish a Dy-nasty."

"You'll be cut to pieces before you're fifty miles across the Border," I said. "You have to travel through Afghanistan to get to that coun-try. It's one mass of mountains and peaks and glaciers, and no Englishman has been through it. The people are utter brutes, and even if you reached them you couldn't do anything."

"That's more like," said Carnehan. "If you could think us a little more mad we would be more pleased. We have come to you to know about this country, to read a book about it, and to be shown maps. We want you to tell us that

we are fools and to show us your books." He
turned to the bookcases.

"Are you at all in earnest?" I said.

"A little," said Dravot, sweetly. "As big a
map as you have got, even if it's all blank where
Kafiristan is, and any books you've got. We
can read, though we aren't very educated."

I uncased the big thirty-two-miles-to-the-inch
map of India, and two smaller Frontier maps,
hauled down volume INF-KAN of the *Encyclopædia Brittanica*, and the men consulted them.

"See here!" said Dravot, his thumb on the
map. "Up to Jagdallak, Peachey and me know
the road. We was there with Roberts's Army.
We'll have to turn off to the right at Jagdallak
through Laghmann territory. Then we get
among the hills—fourteen thousand feet—fifteen
thousand—it will be cold work there, but it don't
look very far on the map."

I handed him Wood on the *Sources of the
Oxus*. Carnehan was deep in the *Encyclopædia*.

"They're a mixed lot," said Dravot, reflec-
tively; "and it won't help us to know the names
of their tribes. The more tribes the more they'll
fight, and the better for us. From Jagdallak to
Ashang. H'mm!"

"But all the information about the country is
as sketchy and inaccurate as can be," I protested.
"No one knows anything about it really. Here's

the file of the *United Services' Institute*. Read what Bellew says."

"Blow Bellew!" said Carnehan. "Dan, they're an all-fired lot of heathens, but this book here says they think they're related to us English."

I smoked while the men pored over *Raverty, Wood*, the maps and the *Encyclopædia*.

"There is no use your waiting," said Dravot, politely. "It's about four o'clock now. We'll go before six o'clock if you want to sleep, and we won't steal any of the papers. Don't you sit up. We're two harmless lunatics, and if you come, to-morrow evening, down to the Serai we'll say good-bye to you."

"You *are* two fools," I answered. "You'll be turned back at the Frontier or cut up the minute you set foot in Afghanistan. Do you want any money or a recommendation down-country? I can help you to the chance of work next week."

"Next week we shall be hard at work ourselves, thank you," said Dravot. "It isn't so easy being a King as it looks. When we've got our Kingdom in going order we'll let you know, and you can come up and help us to govern it."

"Would two lunatics make a Contrack like that?" said Carnehan, with subdued pride, showing me a greasy half-sheet of note-paper on which was written the following. I copied it, then and there, as a curiosity:

This Contract between me and you persuing witnesseth in the name of God—Amen and so forth.

(_One_)   _That me and you will settle this matter together: i. e., to be Kings of Kafiristan._

(_Two_)   _That you and me will not, while this matter is being settled, look at any Liquor, nor any Woman, black, white or brown, so as to get mixed up with one or the other harmful._

(_Three_)   _That we conduct ourselves with dignity and discretion, and if one of us gets into trouble the other will stay by him._

Signed by you and me this day.

Peachey Taliaferro Carnehan.

Daniel Dravot.

Both Gentlemen at Large.

"There was no need for the last article," said Carnehan, blushing modestly; "but it looks regular. Now you know the sort of men that loafers are—we _are_ loafers, Dan, until we get out of India—and _do_ you think that we would sign a Contrack like that unless we was in earnest? We have kept away from the two things that make life worth having."

"You won't enjoy your lives much longer if

you are going to try this idiotic adventure. Don't set the office on fire," I said, "and go away before nine o'clock."

I left them still poring over the maps and making notes on the back of the "Contrack." "Be sure to come down to the Serai to-morrow," were their parting words.

The Kumharsen Serai is the great four-square sink of humanity where the strings of camels and horses from the North load and unload. All the nationalities of Central Asia may be found there, and most of the folk of India proper. Balkh and Bokhara there meet Bengal and Bombay, and try to draw eye-teeth. You can buy ponies, turquoises, Persian pussy-cats, saddle-bags, fat-tailed sheep and musk in the Kumharsen Serai, and get many strange things for nothing. In the afternoon I went down there to see whether my friends intended to keep their word or were lying about drunk.

A priest attired in fragments of ribbons and rags stalked up to me, gravely twisting a child's paper whirligig. Behind him was his servant bending under the load of a crate of mud toys. The two were loading up two camels, and the inhabitants of the Serai watched them with shrieks of laughter.

"The priest is mad," said a horse-dealer to me. "He is going up to Kabul to sell toys to the Amir.

He will either be raised to honor or have his head cut off. He came in here this morning and has been behaving madly ever since."

"The witless are under the protection of God," stammered a flat-cheeked Usbeg in broken Hindi. "They foretell future events."

"Would they could have foretold that my caravan would have been cut up by the Shinwaris almost within shadow of the Pass!" grunted the Eusufzai agent of a Rajputana trading-house whose goods had been feloniously diverted into the hands of other robbers just across the Border, and whose misfortunes were the laughing-stock of the bazar. "Ohé, priest, whence come you and whither do you go?"

"From Roum have I come," shouted the priest, waving his whirligig; "from Roum, blown by the breath of a hundred devils across the sea! O thieves, robbers, liars, the blessing of Pir Khan on pigs, dogs, and perjurers! Who will take the Protected of God to the North to sell charms that are never still to the Amir? The camels shall not gall, the sons shall not fall sick, and the wives shall remain faithful while they are away, of the men who give me place in their caravan. Who will assist me to slipper the King of the Roos with a golden slipper with a silver heel? The protection of Pir Khan be upon his labors!" He spread out the skirts of his gaberdine and pirouetted between the lines of tethered horses.

"There starts a caravan from Peshawur to Kabul in twenty days, *Huzrut*," said the Eusufzai trader. "My camels go therewith. Do thou also go and bring us good-luck."

"I will go even now!" shouted the priest. "I will depart upon my winged camels, and be at Pashawur in a day! Ho! Hazar Mir Khan," he yelled to his servant, "drive out the camels, but let me first mount my own."

He leaped on the back of his beast as it knelt, and, turning round to me, cried:—"Come thou also, Sahib, a little along the road, and I will sell thee a charm—an amulet that shall make thee King of Kafiristan."

Then the light broke upon me, and I followed the two camels out of the Serai till we reached open road and the priest halted.

"What d' you think o' that?" said he in English. "Carnehan can't talk their patter, so I've made him my servant. He makes a handsome servant. 'Tisn't for nothing that I've been knocking about the country for fourteen years. Didn't I do that talk neat? We'll hitch on to a caravan at Peshawur till we get to Jagdallak, and then we'll see if we can get donkeys for our camels, and strike into Kafiristan. Whirligigs for the Amir, O Lor! Put your hand under the camel-bags and tell me what you feel."

I felt the butt of a Martini, and another and another.

"Twenty of 'em," said Dravot, placidly. "Twenty of 'em, and ammunition to correspond, under the whirligigs and the mud dolls."

"Heaven help you if you are caught with those things!" I said. "A Martini is worth her weight in silver among the Pathans."

"Fifteen hundred rupees of capital—every rupee we could beg, borrow, or steal—are invested on these two camels," said Dravot. "We won't get caught. We're going through the Khaiber with a regular caravan. Who'd touch a poor mad priest?"

"Have you got everything you want?" I asked, overcome with astonishment.

"Not yet, but we shall soon. Give us a memento of your kindness, *Brother*. You did me a service yesterday, and that time in Marwar. Half my Kingdom shall you have, as the saying is." I slipped a small charm compass from my watch-chain and handed it up to the priest.

"Good-bye," said Dravot, giving me hand cautiously. "It's the last time we'll shake hands with an Englishman these many days. Shake hands with him, Carnehan," he cried, as the second camel passed me.

Carnehan leaned down and shook hands. Then the camels passed away along the dusty road, and I was left alone to wonder. My eye could detect no failure in the disguises. The scene in Serai attested that they were complete to the native mind. There was just the chance, therefore, that Carnehan and Dravot would be able to wander through Afghanistan without detection. But, beyond, they would find death, certain and awful death.

Ten days later a native friend of mine, giving me the news of the day from Peshawur, wound up his letter with:—"There has been much laughter here on account of a certain mad priest who is going in his estimation to sell petty gauds and insignificant trinkets which he ascribes as great charms to H. H. the Amir of Bokhara. He passed through Peshawur and associated himself to the Second Summer caravan that goes to Kabul. The merchants are pleased because through superstition they imagine that such mad fellows bring good-fortune."

The two, then, were beyond the Border. I would have prayed for them, but, that night, a real King died in Europe, and demanded on obituary notice.

* * * * * *

The wheel of the world swings through the

same phases again and again. Summer passed and winter thereafter, and came and passed again. The daily paper continued and I with it, and upon the third summer there fell a hot night, a night-issue, and a strained waiting for something to be telegraphed from the other side of the world, exactly as had happened before. A few great men had died in the past two years, the machines worked with more clatter, and some of the trees in the Office garden were a few feet taller. But that was all the difference.

I passed over to the press-room, and went through just such a scene as I have already described. The nervous tension was stronger than it had been two years before, and I felt the heat more acutely. At three o'clock I cried, "Print off," and turned to go, when there crept to my chair what was left of a man. He was bent into a circle, his head was sunk between his shoulders, and he moved his feet one over the other like a bear. I could hardly see whether he walked or crawled—this rag-wrapped, whining cripple who addressed me by name, crying that he was come back. "Can you give me a drink?" he whimpered. "For the Lord's sake, give me a drink!"

I went back to the office, the man following with groans of pain, and I turned up the lamp.

"Don't you know me?" he gasped, dropping

into a chair, and he turned his drawn face, surmounted by a shock of grey hair, to the light.

I looked at him intently. Once before had I seen eyebrows that met over the nose in an inch-broad black band, but for the life of me I could not tell where.

"I don't know you," I said, handing him the whiskey. "What can I do for you?"

He took a gulp of the spirit raw, and shivered in spite of the suffocating heat.

"I've come back," he repeated; "and I was the King of Kafiristan—me and Dravot—crowned Kings we was! In this office we settled it—you setting there and giving us the books. I am Peachey—Peachey Taliaferro Carnehan, and you've been setting here ever since—O Lord!"

I was more than a little astonished, and expressed my feelings accordingly.

"It's true," said Carnehan, with a dry cackle, nursing his feet, which were wrapped in rags. "True as gospel. Kings we were, with crowns upon our heads—me and Dravot—poor Dan—oh, poor, poor Dan, that would never take advice, not though I begged of him!"

"Take the whiskey," I said, "and take your own time. Tell me all you can recollect of everything from beginning to end. You got across the border on your camels, Dravot dressed as a mad priest and you his servant. Do you remember that?"

"I ain't mad—yet, but I shall be that way soon. Of course I remember. Keep looking at me, or maybe my words will go all to pieces. Keep looking at me in my eyes and don't say anything."

I leaned forward and looked into his face as steadily as I could. He dropped one hand upon the table and I grasped it by the wrist. It was twisted like a bird's claw, and upon the back was a ragged, red, diamond-shaped scar.

"No, don't look there. Look at *me*," said Carnehan.

"That comes afterward, but for the Lord's sake don't distrack me. We left with that caravan, me and Dravot playing all sorts of antics to amuse the people we were with. Dravot used to make us laugh in the evenings when all the people was cooking their dinners—cooking their dinners, and . . . what did they do then? They lit little fires with sparks that went into Dravot's beard, and we all laughed—fit to die. Little red fires they was, going into Dravot's big red beard—so funny." His eyes left mine and he smiled foolishly.

"You went as far as Jagdallak with that caravan," I said, at a venture, "after you had lit those fires. To Jagdallah, where you turned off to try to get into Kafiristan."

"No, we didn't neither. What are you talking about? We turned off before Jagdallak, because we heard the roads was good. But they wasn't good enough for our two camels—mine and Dravot's. When we left the caravan, Dravot took off all his clothes and mine too, and said we would be heathen, because the Kafirs didn't allow Mohammedans to talk to them. So we dressed betwixt and between, and such a sight as Daniel Dravot I never saw yet nor expect to see again. He burned half his beard, and slung a sheep-skin over his shoulder, and shaved his head into patterns. He shaved mine, too, and made me wear outrageous things to look like a heathen. That was in a most mountaineous country, and our camels couldn't go along any more because of the mountains. They were tall and black, and coming home I saw them fight like wild goats—there are lots of goats in Kafiristan. And these mountains, they never keep still, no more than the goats. Always fighting they are, and don't let you sleep at night."

"Take some more whiskey," I said, very slowly. "What did you and Daniel Dravot do when the camels could go no further because of the rough roads that led into Kafiristan?"

"What did which do? There was a party called Peachey Taliaferro Carnehan that was with Dravot. Shall I tell you about him? He died out there in the cold. Slap from the bridge fell old Peachey, turning and twisting in the air like a penny whirligig that you can sell to the Amir. —No; they was two for three ha'pence, those whirligigs, or I am much mistaken and woful sore. And then these camels were no use, and Peachey said to Dravot—'For the Lord's sake, let's get out of this before our heads are chopped off,' and with that they killed the camels all among the mountains, not having anything in particular to eat, but first they took off the boxes with the guns and the ammunition, till two men came along driving four mules. Dravot up and dances in front of them, singing,—'Sell me four mules.' Says the first man,—'If you are rich enough to buy, you are rich enough to rob;' but before ever he could put his hand to his knife, Dravot breaks his neck over his knee, and the other party runs away. So Carnehan loaded the mules with the rifles that was taken off the camels, and together we starts forward into those bitter cold mountaineous parts, and never a road broader than the back of your hand."

He paused for a moment, while I asked him if he could remember the nature of the country through which he had journeyed.

"I am telling you as straight as I can, but my head isn't as good as it might be. They drove nails through it to make me hear better how

Dravot died. The country was mountaineous
and the mules were most contrary, and the inhabitants was dispersed and solitary. They went up
and up, and down and down, and that other
party, Carnehan, was imploring of Dravot not to
sing and whistle so loud, for fear of bringing
down the tremenjus avalanches. But Dravot says
that if a King couldn't sing it wasn't worth being
King, and whacked the mules over the rump, and
never took no heed for ten cold days. We came
to a big level valley all among the mountains, and
the mules were near dead, so we killed them, not
having anything in special for them or us to eat.
We sat upon the boxes, and played odd and even
with the cartridges that was jolted out.

"Then ten men with bows and arrows ran
down that valley, chasing twenty men with bows
and arrows, and the row was tremenjus. They
was fair men—fairer than you or me—with
yellow hair and remarkable well built. Says
Dravot, unpacking the guns—'This is the beginning of the business. We'll fight for the ten
men,' and with that he fires two rifles at the
twenty men, and drops one of them at two
hundred yards from the rock where we was sitting. The other men began to run, but Carnehan
and Dravot sits on the boxes picking them off at
all ranges, up and down the valley. Then we
goes up to the ten men that had run across the

snow too, and they fires a footy little arrow at us. Dravot he shoots above their heads and they all falls down flat. Then he walks over them and kicks them, and then he lifts them up and shakes hands all round to make them friendly like. He calls them and gives them the boxes to carry, and waves his hand for all the world as though he was King already. They takes the boxes and him across the valley and up the hill into a pine wood on the top, where there was half a dozen big stone idols. Dravot he goes to the biggest—a fellow they call Imbra—and lays a rifle and a cartridge at his feet, rubbing his nose respectful with his own nose, patting him on the head, and saluting in front of it. He turns round to the men and nods his head, and says,—'That's all right. I'm in the know too, and all these old jim-jams are my friends.' Then he opens his mouth and points down it, and when the first man brings him food, he says—'No;' and when the second man brings him food, he says—'No;' but when one of the old priests and the boss of the village brings him food, he says—'Yes;' very haughty, and eats it slow. That was how we came to our first village, without any trouble, just as though we had tumbled from the skies. But we tumbled from one of those damned rope-bridges, you see, and you couldn't expect a man to laugh much after that."

"Take some more whiskey and go on," I said.
"That was the first village you came into. How
did you get to be King?"

"I wasn't King," said Carnehan. "Dravot he
was the King, and a handsome man he looked
with the gold crown on his head and all. Him
and the other party stayed in that village, and
every morning Dravot sat by the side of old
Imbra, and the people came and worshipped.
That was Dravot's order. Then a lot of men
came into the valley, and Carnehan and Dravot
picks them off with the rifles before they knew
where they was, and runs down into the valley
and up again the other side, and finds another
village, same as the first one, and the people all
falls down flat on their faces, and Dravot says,—
'Now what is the trouble between you two villages?' and the people points to a woman, as
fair as you or me, that was carried off, and
Dravot takes her back to the first village and
counts up the dead—eight there was. For each
dead man Dravot pours a little milk on the
ground and waves his arms like a whirligig
and 'That's all right,' says he. Then he and
Carnehan takes the big boss of each village by
the arm and walks them down into the valley,
and shows them how to scratch a line with a
spear right down the valley, and gives each a sod
of turf from both sides o' the line. Then all the

people comes down and shouts like the devil and all, and Dravot says,—'Go and dig the land, and be fruitful and multiply,' which they did, though they didn't understand. Then we asks the names of things in their lingo—bread and water and fire and idols and such, and Dravot leads the priest of each village up to the idol, and says he must sit there and judge the people, and if anything goes wrong he is to be shot.

"Next week they was all turning up the land in the valley as quiet as bees and much prettier, and the priests heard all the complaints and told Dravot in dumb show what it was about. 'That's just the beginning,' says Dravot. 'They think we're Gods.' He and Carnehan picks out twenty good men and shows them how to click off a rifle, and form fours, and advance in line, and they was very pleased to do so, and clever to see the hang of it. Then he takes out his pipe and his baccy-pouch and leaves one at one village and one at the other, and off we two goes to see what was to be done in the next valley. That was all rock, and there was a little village there, and Carnehan says,—'Send 'em to the old valley to plant,' and takes 'em there and gives 'em some land that wasn't took before. They were a poor lot, and we blooded 'em with a kid before letting 'em into the new Kingdom. That was to impress the people, and then they settled down

quiet, and Carnehan went back to Dravot who
had got into another valley, all snow and ice and
most mountaineous. There was no people there
and the Army got afraid, so Dravot shoots one of
them, and goes on till he finds some people in a
village, and the Army explains that unless the
people wants to be killed they had better not
shoot their little matchlocks; for they had matchlocks. We makes friends with the priest and I
stays there alone with two of the Army, teaching
the men how to drill, and a thundering big Chief
comes across the snow with kettle-drums and
horns twanging, because he heard there was a
new God kicking about. Carnehan sights for
the brown of the men half a mile across the
snow and wings one of them. Then he sends a
message to the Chief that, unless he wished to be
killed, he must come and shake hands with me
and leave his arms behind. The chief comes
alone first, and Carnehan shakes hands with him
and whirls his arms about, same as Dravot used,
and very much surprised that Chief was, and
strokes my eyebrows. Then Carnehan goes
alone to the Chief, and asks him in dumb show
if he had an enemy he hated. 'I have,' says the
Chief. So Carnehan weeds out the pick of his
men, and sets the two of the Army to show
them drill and at the end of two weeks the men
can manœuvre about as well as Volunteers. So

he marches with the Chief to a great big plain on the top of a mountain, and the Chief's men rushes into a village and takes it; we three Martinis firing into the brown of the enemy. So we took that village too, and I gives the Chief a rag from my coat and says, 'Occupy till I come:' which was scriptural. By way of a reminder, when me and the Army was eighteen hundred yards away, I drops a bullet near him standing on the snow, and all the people falls flat on their faces. Then I sends a letter to Dravot, wherever he be by land or by sea."

At the risk of throwing the creature out of train I interrupted,—"How could you write a letter up yonder?"

"The letter?—Oh!—The letter! Keep looking at me between the eyes, please. It was a string-talk letter, that we'd learned the way of it from a blind beggar in the Punjab."

I remember that there had once come to the office a blind man with a knotted twig and a piece of string which he wound round the twig according to some cypher of his own. He could, after the lapse of days or hours, repeat the sentence which he had reeled up. He had reduced the alphabet to eleven primitive sounds; and tried to teach me his method, but failed.

"I sent that letter to Dravot," said Carnehan; "and told him to come back because this Kingdom was growing too big for me to handle, and then I struck for the first valley, to see how the priests were working. They called the village we took along with the Chief, Bashkai, and the first village we took, Er-Heb. The priests at Er-Heb was doing all right, but they had a lot of pending cases about land to show me, and some men from another village had been firing arrows at night. I went out and looked for that village and fired four rounds at it from a thousand yards. That used all the cartridges I cared to spend, and I waited for Dravot, who had been away two or three months, and I kept my people quiet.

"One morning I heard the devil's own noise of drums and horns, and Dan Dravot marches down the hill with his Army and a tail of hundreds of men, and, which was the most amazing —a great gold crown on his head. 'My Gord, Carnehan,' says Daniel, 'this is a tremenjus business, and we've got the whole country as far as it's worth having. I am the son of Alexander by Queen Semiramis, and you're my younger brother and a God too! It's the biggest thing we've ever seen. I've been marching and fighting for six weeks with the Army, and every footy little village for fifty miles has come in rejoiceful; and more than that, I've got the key of the whole show, as you'll see, and I've got a

crown for you! I told 'em to make two of 'em
at a place called Shu, where the gold lies in the
rock like suet in mutton. Gold I've seen, and
turquoise I've kicked out of the cliffs, and there's
garnets in the sands of the river, and here's a
chunk of amber that a man brought me. Call up
all the priests and, here, take your crown.'

"One of the men opens a black hair bag and I
slips the crown on. It was too small and too
heavy, but I wore it for the glory. Hammered
gold it was—five pound weight, like a hoop of a
barrel.

"'Peachey,' says Dravot, 'we don't want to
fight no more. The Craft's the trick so help me!'
and he brings forward that same Chief that I left
at Bashkai—Billy Fish we called him afterward,
because he was so like Billy Fish that drove the
big tank-engine at Mach on the Bolan in the old
days. 'Shake hands with him,' says Dravot, and
I shook hands and nearly dropped, for Billy Fish
gave me the Grip. I said nothing, but tried him
with the Fellow Craft Grip. He answers, all
right, and I tried the Master's Grip, but that was
a slip. 'A Fellow Craft he is!' I says to Dan.
'Does he know the word?' 'He does,' says
Dan, 'and all the priests know. It's a miracle!
The Chiefs and the priests can work a Fellow
Craft Lodge in a way that's very like ours, and
they've cut the marks on the rocks, but they

don't know the Third Degree, and they've come
to find out. It's Gord's Truth. I've known these
long years that the Afghans knew up to the
Fellow Craft Degree, but this is a miracle. A
God and a Grand-Master of the Craft am I, and a
Lodge in the Third Degree I will open, and we'll
raise the head priests and the Chiefs of the villages.'

"'It's against all the law,' I says, 'holding a
Lodge without warrant from any one; and we
never held office in any Lodge.'

"'It's a master-stroke of policy,' says Dravot.
'It means running the country as easy as a four-
wheeled bogy on a down grade. We can't stop
to inquire now, or they'll turn against us. I've
forty Chiefs at my heel, and passed and raised
according to their merit they shall be. Billet
these men on the villages and see that we run up
a Lodge of some kind. The temple of Imbra
will do for the Lodge-room. The women must
make aprons as you show them. I'll hold a
levee of Chiefs to-night and Lodge to-morrow.'

"I was fair run off my legs, but I wasn't such
a fool as not to see what a pull this Craft business gave us. I showed the priests' families
how to make aprons of the degrees, but for
Dravot's apron the blue border and marks was
made of turquoise lumps on white hide, not
cloth. We took a great square stone in the tem-

ple for the Master's chair, and little stones for
the officers' chairs, and painted the black pave-
ment with white squares, and did what we could
to make things regular.

"At the levee which was held that night on
the hillside with big bonfires, Dravot gives out
that him and me were Gods and sons of Alexander, and Past Grand-Masters in the Craft, and
was come to make Kafiristan a country where
every man should eat in peace and drink in quiet,
and specially obey us. Then the Chiefs come
round to shake hands, and they was so hairy
and white and fair it was just shaking hands with
old friends. We gave them names according as
they was like men we had known in India—Billy
Fish, Holly Dilworth, Pikky Kergan that was
Bazar-master when I was at Mhow, and so on
and so on.

"*The* most amazing miracle was at Lodge next
night. One of the old priests was watching us
continuous, and I felt uneasy, for I knew we'd
have to fudge the Ritual, and I didn't know what
the men knew. The old priest was a stranger
come in from beyond the village of Bashkai.
The minute Dravot puts on the Master's apron
that the girls had made for him, the priest fetches
a whoop and a howl, and tries to overturn the
stone that Dravot was sitting on. 'It's all up
now,' I says. 'That comes of meddling with the

Craft without warrant!' Dravot never winked
an eye, not when ten priests took and tilted over
the Grand-Master's chair—which was to say the
stone of Imbra. The priest begins rubbing the
bottom end of it to clear away the black dirt,
and presently he shows all the other priests the
Master's Mark, same as was on Dravot's apron,
cut into the stone. Not even the priests of the
temple of Imbra knew it was there. The old
chap falls flat on his face at Dravot's feet and
kisses 'em. 'Luck again,' says Dravot, across the
Lodge to me, 'they say it's the missing Mark
that no one could understand the why of. We're
more than safe now.' Then he bangs the butt
of his gun for a gavel and says:—' By virtue of
the authority vested in me by my own right hand
and the help of Peachey, I declare myself Grand-
Master of all Freemasonry in Kafiristan in this the
Mother Lodge o' the country, and King of Kafiristan equally with Peachey!' At that he puts on
his crown and I puts on mine—I was doing Senior
Warden—and we opens the Lodge in most ample
form. It was a amazing miracle! The priests
moved in Lodge through the first two degrees
almost without telling, as if the memory was
coming back to them. After that, Peachey and
Dravot raised such as was worthy—high priests
and Chiefs of far-off villages. Billy Fish was the
first, and I can tell you we scared the soul out of

him. It was not in any way according to Ritual, but it served our turn. We didn't raise more than ten of the biggest men because we didn't want to make the Degree common. And they was clamoring to be raised.

" 'In another six months,' says Dravot, 'we'll hold another Communication and see how you are working.' Then he asks them about their villages, and learns that they was fighting one against the other and were fair sick and tired of it. And when they wasn't doing that they was fighting with the Mohammedans. ' You can fight those when they come into our country,' says Dravot. 'Tell off every tenth man of your tribes for a Frontier guard, and send two hundred at a time to this valley to be drilled. Nobody is going to be shot or speared any more so long as he does well, and I know that you won't cheat me because you're white people—sons of Alexander— and not like common, black Mohammedans. You are *my* people and by God,' says he, running off into English at the end—'I'll make a damned fine Nation of you, or I'll die in the making!'

"I can't tell all we did for the next six months because Dravot did a lot I couldn't see the hang of, and he learned their lingo in a way I never could. My work was to help the people plough, and now and again go out with some of the Army and see what the other villages were doing,

and make 'em throw rope-bridges across the ra-
vines which cut up the country horrid. Dravot
was very kind to me, but when he walked up
and down in the pine wood pulling that bloody
red beard of his with both fists I knew he was
thinking plans I could not advise him about, and
I just waited for orders.

"But Dravot never showed me disrespect before the people. They were afraid of me and the
Army, but they loved Dan. He was the best of
friends with the priests and the Chiefs; but any
one could come across the hills with a complaint
and Dravot would hear him out fair, and call
four priests together and say what was to be
done. He used to call in Billy Fish from Bashkai,
and Pikky Kergan from Shu, and an old Chief
we called Kafuzelum—it was like enough to his
real name—and hold councils with 'em when
there was any fighting to be done in small villages. That was his Council of War, and the
four priests of Bashkai, Shu, Khawak, and Ma-
dora was his Privy Council. Between the lot of
'em they sent me, with forty men and twenty
rifles, and sixty men carrying turquoises, into the
Ghorband country to buy those hand-made Martini rifles, that come out of the Amir's workshops
at Kabul, from one of the Amir's Herati regiments that would have sold the very teeth out of
their mouths for turquoises.

"I stayed in Ghorband a month, and gave the Governor there the pick of my baskets for hush-money, and bribed the Colonel of the regiment some more, and, between the two and the tribespeople, we got more than a hundred hand-made Martinis, a hundred good Kohat Jezails that'll throw to six hundred yards, and forty man-loads of very bad ammunition for the rifles. I came back with what I had, and distributed 'em among the men that the Chiefs sent to me to drill. Dravot was too busy to attend to those things, but the old Army that we first made helped me, and we turned out five hundred men that could drill, and two hundred that knew how to hold arms pretty straight. Even those cork-screwed, hand-made guns was a miracle to them. Dravot talked big about powder-shops and factories, walking up and down in the pine wood when the winter was coming on.

"'I won't make a Nation,' says he. 'I'll make an Empire! These men aren't niggers; they're English! Look at their eyes—look at their mouths. Look at the way they stand up. They sit on chairs in their own houses. They're the Lost Tribes, or something like it, and they've grown to be English. I'll take a census in the spring if the priests don't get frightened. There must be a fair two million of 'em in these hills. The villages are full o' little children. Two mil-

lion people—two hundred and fifty thousand
fighting men—and all English! They only want
the rifles and a little drilling. Two hundred and
fifty thousand men, ready to cut in on Russia's
right flank when she tries for India! Peachey,
man,' he says, chewing his beard in great hunks,
' we shall be Emperors—Emperors of the Earth!
Rajah Brooke will be a suckling to us. I'll treat
with the Viceroy on equal terms. I'll ask him to
send me twelve picked English—twelve that I
know of—to help us govern a bit. There's
Mackray, Sergeant-pensioner at Segowli—many's
the good dinner he's given me, and his wife a
pair of trousers. There's Donkin, the Warder of
Tounghoo Jail; there's hundreds that I could lay
my hand on if I was in India. The Viceroy shall
do it for me. I'll send a man through in the
spring for those men, and I'll write for a dispen-
sation from the Grand Lodge for what I've done
as Grand-Master. That—and all the Sniders
that'll be thrown out when the native troops in
India take up the Martini. They'll be worn
smooth, but they'll do for fighting in these hills.
Twelve English, a hundred thousand Sniders run
through the Amir's country in driblets—I'd be
content with twenty thousand in one year—and
we'd be an Empire. When everything was
shipshape, I'd hand over the crown—this crown
I'm wearing now—to Queen Victoria on my

knees, and she'd say: "Rise up, Sir Daniel Dravot." Oh, it's big! It's big, I tell you! But there's so much to be done in every place— Bashkai, Khawak, Shu, and everywhere else.'

"'What is it?' I says. 'There are no more men coming in to be drilled this autumn. Look at those fat, black clouds. They're bringing the snow.'

"'It isn't that,' says Daniel, putting his hand very hard on my shoulder; 'and I don't wish to say anything that's against you, for no other living man would have followed me and made me what I am as you have done. You're a first-class Commander-in-Chief, and the people know you; but—it's a big country, and somehow you can't help me, Peachey, in the way I want to be helped.'

"'Go to your blasted priests, then!' I said, and I was sorry when I made that remark, but it did hurt me sore to find Daniel talking so superior when I'd drilled all the men, and done all he told me.

"'Don't let's quarrel, Peachey,' says Daniel, without cursing. 'You're a King too, and the half of this Kingdom is yours; but can't you see, Peachey, we want cleverer men than us now— three or four of 'em, that we can scatter about for our Deputies. It's a hugeous great State, and I can't always tell the right thing to do, and I

haven't time for all I want to do, and here's the
winter coming on and all.' He put half his beard
into his mouth, and it was as red as the gold of
his crown.

"'I'm sorry, Daniel,' says I. 'I've done all I
could. I've drilled the men and shown the
people how to stack their oats better; and I've
brought in those tinware rifles from Ghorband—
but I know what you're driving at. I take it
Kings always feel oppressed that way.'

"'There's another thing too,' says Dravot,
walking up and down. 'The winter's coming
and these people won't be giving much trouble,
and if they do we can't move about. I want a
wife.'

"'For Gord's sake leave the women alone!'
I says. 'We've both got all the work we can,
though I *am* a fool. Remember the Contrack,
and keep clear o' women.'

"'The Contrack only lasted till such time as
we was Kings; and Kings we have been these
months past,' says Dravot, weighing his crown
in his hand. 'You go get a wife too, Peachey—
a nice, strappin', plump girl that'll keep you
warm in the winter. They're prettier than
English girls, and we can take the pick of 'em.
Boil 'em once or twice in hot water, and they'll
come as fair as chicken and ham.'

"'Don't tempt me!' I says. 'I will not have

any dealings with a woman not till we are a dam' side more settled than we are now. I've been doing the work o' two men, and you've been doing the work o' three. Let's lie off a bit, and see if we can get some better tobacco from Afghan country and run in some good liquor; but no women.'

"'Who's talking o' *women*?' says Dravot. 'I said *wife*—a Queen to breed a King's son for the King. A Queen out of the strongest tribe, that'll make them your blood-brothers, and that'll lie by your side and tell you all the people thinks about you and their own affairs. That's what I want.'

"'Do you remember that Bengali woman I kept at Mogul Serai when I was a plate-layer?' says I. 'A fat lot o' good she was to me. She taught me the lingo and one or two other things; but what happened? She ran away with the Station Master's servant and half my month's pay. Then she turned up at Dadur Junction in tow of a half-caste, and had the impidence to say I was her husband—all among the drivers in the running-shed!'

"'We've done with that,' says Dravot. 'These women are whiter than you or me, and a Queen I will have for the winter months.'

"'For the last time o' asking, Dan, do *not*,' I says. 'It'll only bring us harm. The Bible says that Kings ain't to waste their strength on women, 'specially when they've got a new raw Kingdom to work over.'

" 'For the last time of answering I will,' said Dravot, and he went away through the pine-trees looking like a big red devil. The low sun hit his crown and beard on one side and the two blazed like hot coals.

"But getting a wife was not as easy as Dan thought. He put it before the Council, and there was no answer till Billy Fish said that he'd better ask the girls. Dravot damned them all round. 'What's wrong with me?' he shouts, standing by the idol Imbra. 'Am I a dog or am I not enough of a man for your wenches? Haven't I put the shadow of my hand over this country? Who stopped the last Afghan raid?' It was me really, but Dravot was too angry to remember. 'Who brought your guns? Who repaired the bridges? Who's the Grand-Master of the sign cut in the stone?' and he thumped his hand on the block that he used to sit on in Lodge, and at Council, which opened like Lodge always. Billy Fish said nothing and no more did the others. 'Keep your hair on, Dan,' said I; 'and ask the girls. That's how it's done at Home, and these people are quite English.'

" 'The marriage of the King is a matter of State,' says Dan, in a white-hot rage, for he could feel, I hope, that he was going against his better mind. He walked out of the Council-room, and the others sat still, looking at the ground.

"'Billy Fish,' says I to the Chief of Bashkai, 'what's the difficulty here? A straight answer to a true friend.' 'You know,' says Billy Fish. 'How should a man tell you who know every-thing? How can daughters of men marry Gods or Devils? It's not proper.'

"I remembered something like that in the Bible; but if, after seeing us as long as they had, they still believed we were Gods, it wasn't for me to undeceive them.

"'A God can do anything,' says I. 'If the King is fond of a girl he'll not let her die.' 'She'll have to,' said Billy Fish. 'There are all sorts of Gods and Devils in these mountains, and now and again a girl marries one of them and isn't seen any more. Besides, you two know the Mark cut in the stone. Only the Gods know that. We thought you were men till you showed the sign of the Master.'

"I wished then that we had explained about the loss of the genuine secrets of a Master-Mason at the first go-off; but I said nothing. All that night there was a blowing of horns in a little dark temple half-way down the hill, and I heard a girl crying fit to die. One of the priests told us that she was being prepared to marry the King.

"'I'll have no nonsense of that kind,' says Dan. 'I don't want to interfere with your customs, but I'll take my own wife.' 'The girl's a little bit afraid,' says the priest. 'She thinks she's going to die, and they are a-heartening of her up down in the temple.'

"'Hearten her very tender, then,' says Dravot, 'or I'll hearten you with the butt of a gun so that you'll never want to be heartened again.' He licked his lips, did Dan, and stayed up walking about more than half the night, thinking of the wife that he was going to get in the morning. I wasn't any means comfortable, for I knew that dealings with a woman in foreign parts, though you was a crowned King twenty times over, could not but be risky. I got up very early in the morning while Dravot was asleep, and I saw the priests talking together in whispers, and the Chiefs talking together too, and they looked at me out of the corners of their eyes.

"'What is up, Fish?' I says to the Bashkai man, who was wrapped up in his furs and looking splendid to behold.

"'I can't rightly say,' says he; 'but if you can induce the King to drop all this nonsense about marriage, you'll be doing him and me and yourself a great service.'

"'That I do believe,' says I. 'But sure, you

know, Billy, as well as me, having fought against
and for us, that the King and me are nothing
more than two of the finest men that God Al-
mighty ever made. Nothing more, I do assure
you.'

"'That may be,' says Billy Fish, 'and yet I
should be sorry if it was.' He sinks his head
upon his great fur cloak for a minute and thinks.
'King,' says he, 'be you man or God or Devil,
I'll stick by you to-day. I have twenty of my
men with me, and they will follow me. We'll
go to Bashkai until the storm blows over.'

"A little snow had fallen in the night, and
everything was white except the greasy fat
clouds that blew down and down from the north.
Dravot came out with his crown on his head,
swinging his arms and stamping his feet, and
looking more pleased than Punch.

"'For the last time, drop it, Dan,' says I, in a
whisper. 'Billy Fish here says that there will be
a row.'

"'A row among my people!' says Dravot.
'Not much. Peachey, you're a fool not to get a
wife too. Where's the girl?' says he, with a
voice as loud as the braying of a jackass. 'Call
up all the Chiefs and priests, and let the Emperor
see if his wife suits him.'

"There was no need to call any one. They
were all there leaning on their guns and spears

round the clearing in the centre of the pine wood.
A deputation of priests went down to the little
temple to bring up the girl, and the horns blew
up fit to wake the dead. Billy Fish saunters
round and gets as close to Daniel as he could,
and behind him stood his twenty men with
matchlocks. Not a man of them under six feet.
I was next to Dravot, and behind me was twenty
men of the regular Army. Up comes the girl,
and a strapping wench she was, covered with
silver and turquoises but white as death, and
looking back every minute at the priests.

"'She'll do,' said Dan, looking her over.
'What's to be afraid of, lass? Come and kiss
me.' He puts his arm round her. She shuts her
eyes, gives a bit of a squeak, and down goes her
face in the side of Dan's flaming red beard.

"'The slut's bitten me!' says he, clapping his
hand to his neck, and, sure enough, his hand was
red with blood. Billy Fish and two of his matchlock-men catches hold of Dan by the shoulders
and drags him into the Bashkai lot, while the
priests howls in their lingo,—'Neither God nor
Devil but a man!' I was all taken aback, for a
priest cut at me in front, and the Army behind
began firing into the Bashkai men.

"'God A-mighty!' says Dan. 'What is the
meaning o' this?'

"'Come back! Come away!' says Billy Fish.

'Ruin and Mutiny is the matter. We'll break for Bashkai if we can.'

"I tried to give some sort of orders to my men—the men o' the regular Army—but it was no use, so I fired into the brown of 'em with an English Martini and drilled three beggars in a line. The valley was full of shouting, howling creatures, and every soul was shrieking, 'Not a God nor a Devil but only a man!' The Bashkai troops stuck to Billy Fish all they were worth, but their matchlocks wasn't half as good as the Kabul breech-loaders, and four of them dropped. Dan was bellowing like a bull, for he was very wrathy; and Billy Fish had a hard job to prevent him running out at the crowd.

"'We can't stand,' says Billy Fish. 'Make a run for it down the valley! The whole place is against us.' The matchlock-men ran, and we went down the valley in spite of Dravot's protestations. He was swearing horribly and crying out that he was a King. The priests rolled great stones on us, and the regular Army fired hard, and there wasn't more than six men, not counting Dan, Billy Fish, and Me, that came down to the bottom of the valley alive.

"Then they stopped firing and the horns in the temple blew again. 'Come away—for Gord's sake come away!' says Billy Fish. 'They'll send runners out to all the villages before ever we get to Bashkai. I can protect you there, but I can't do anything now.'

"My own notion is that Dan began to go mad in his head from that hour. He stared up and down like a stuck pig. Then he was all for walking back alone and killing the priests with his bare hands; which he could have done. 'An Emperor am I,' says Daniel, 'and next year I shall be a Knight of the Queen.'

"'All right, Dan,' says I; 'but come along now while there's time.'

"'It's your fault,' says he, 'for not looking after your Army better. There was mutiny in the midst, and you didn't know—you damned engine-driving, plate-laying, missionary's-pass-hunting hound!' He sat upon a rock and called me every foul name he could lay tongue to. I was too heart-sick to care, though it was all his foolishness that brought the smash.

"'I'm sorry, Dan,' says I, 'but there's no accounting for natives. This business is our Fifty-Seven. Maybe we'll make something out of it yet, when we've got to Bashkai.'

"'Let's get to Bashkai, then,' says Dan, 'and, by God, when I come back here again I'll sweep the valley so there isn't a bug in a blanket left!'

"We walked all that day, and all that night Dan was stumping up and down on the snow, chewing his beard and muttering to himself.

"'There's no hope o' getting clear,' said Billy Fish. 'The priests will have sent runners to the villages to say that you are only men. Why didn't you stick on as Gods till things was more settled? I'm a dead man,' says Billy Fish, and he throws himself down on the snow and begins to pray to his Gods.

"Next morning we was in a cruel bad country —all up and down, no level ground at all, and no food either. The six Bashkai men looked at Billy Fish hungry-wise as if they wanted to ask something, but they said never a word. At noon we came to the top of a flat mountain all covered with snow, and when we climbed up into it, behold, there was an Army in position waiting in the middle!

"'The runners have been very quick,' says Billy Fish, with a little bit of a laugh. 'They are waiting for us.'

"Three or four men began to fire from the enemy's side, and a chance shot took Daniel in the calf of the leg. That brought him to his senses. He looks across the snow at the Army, and sees the rifles that we had brought into the country.

"'We're done for,' says he. 'They are Englishmen, these people,—and it's my blasted nonsense that has brought you to this. Get back, Billy Fish, and take your men away; you've

done what you could, and now cut for it. Carnehan,' says he, 'shake hands with me and go
along with Billy. Maybe they won't kill you.
I'll go and meet 'em alone. It's me that did it.
Me, the King!'

"'Go!' says I. 'Go to Hell, Dan. I'm with
you here. Billy Fish, you clear out, and we two
will meet those folk.'

"'I'm a Chief,' says Billy Fish, quite quiet. 'I
stay with you. My men can go.'

"The Bashkai fellows didn't wait for a second
word but ran off, and Dan and Me and Billy Fish
walked across to where the drums were drumming and the horns were horning. It was cold
—awful cold. I've got that cold in the back of
my head now. There's a lump of it there."

The punkah-coolies had gone to sleep. Two
kerosene lamps were blazing in the office, and
the perspiration poured down my face and
splashed on the blotter as I leaned forward.
Carnehan was shivering, and I feared that his
mind might go. I wiped my face, took a fresh
grip of the piteously mangled hands, and said:—
"What happened after that?"

The momentary shift of my eyes had broken
the clear current.

"What was you pleased to say?" whined
Carnehan. "They took them without any
sound. Not a little whisper all along the snow,

not though the King knocked down the first
man that set hand on him—not though old
Peachey fired his last cartridge into the brown of
'em. Not a single solitary sound did those
swines make. They just closed up tight, and I
tell you their furs stunk. There was a man
called Billy Fish, a good friend of us all, and
they cut his throat, Sir, then and there, like a
pig; and the King kicks up the bloody snow and
says:—'We've had a dashed fine run for our
money. What's coming next?' But Peachey,
Peachey Taliaferro, I tell you, Sir, in confidence
as betwixt two friends, he lost his head, Sir.
No, he didn't neither. The King lost his head,
so he did, all along o' one of those cunning rope-
bridges. Kindly let me have the paper-cutter,
Sir. It tilted this way. They marched him a
mile across that snow to a rope-bridge over a
ravine with a river at the bottom. You may
have seen such. They prodded him behind like
an ox. 'Damn your eyes!' says the King.
'D'you suppose I can't die like a gentleman?'
He turns to Peachey—Peachey that was crying
like a child. 'I've brought you to this, Peachey,'
says he. 'Brought you out of your happy life
to be killed in Kafiristan, where you was late
Commander-in-Chief of the Emperor's forces.
Say you forgive me, Peachey.' 'I do,' says
Peachey. 'Fully and freely do I forgive you,

Dan.' 'Shake hands, Peachey,' says he. 'I'm going now.' Out he goes, looking neither right nor left, and when he was plumb in the middle of those dizzy dancing ropes, 'Cut, you beggars,' he shouts; and they cut, and old Dan fell, turning round and round and round twenty thousand miles, for he took half an hour to fall till he struck the water, and I could see his body caught on a rock with the gold crown close beside.

"But do you know what they did to Peachey between two pine trees? They crucified him, Sir, as Peachey's hand will show. They used wooden pegs for his hands and his feet; and he didn't die. He hung there and screamed, and they took him down next day, and said it was a miracle that he wasn't dead. They took him down—poor old Peachey that hadn't done them any harm—that hadn't done them any. . . ."

He rocked to and fro and wept bitterly, wiping his eyes with the back of his scarred hands and moaning like a child for some ten minutes.

"They was cruel enough to feed him up in the temple, because they said he was more of a God than old Daniel that was a man. Then they turned him out on the snow, and told him to go home, and Peachey came home in about a year, begging along the roads quite safe; for Daniel

Dravot he walked before and said:—'Come along, Peachey. It's a big thing we're doing.' The mountains they danced at night, and the mountains they tried to fall on Peachey's head, but Dan he held up his hand, and Peachey came along bent double. He never let go of Dan's hand, and he never let go of Dan's head. They gave it to him as a present in the temple, to remind him not to come again, and though the crown was pure gold, and Peachey was starving, never would Peachey sell the same. You knew Dravot, Sir! You knew Right Worshipful Brother Dravot! Look at him now!"

He fumbled in the mass of rags round his bent waist; brought out a black horsehair bag embroidered with silver thread; and shook therefrom on to my table—the dried, withered head of Daniel Dravot! The morning sun that had long been paling the lamps struck the red beard and blind sunken eyes; struck, too, a heavy circlet of gold studded with raw turquoises, that Carnehan placed tenderly on the battered temples.

"You behold now," said Carnehan, "the Emperor in his habit as he lived—the King of Kafiristan with his crown upon his head. Poor old Daniel that was a monarch once!"

I shuddered, for, in spite of defacements manifold, I recognized the head of the man of Mar-

war Junction.   Carnehan rose to go.   I attempted
to stop him.   He was not fit to walk abroad.
"Let me take away the whiskey, and give me a
little money," he gasped.   "I was a King once.
I'll go to the Deputy Commissioner and ask to set
in the Poorhouse till I get my health.   No, thank
you, I can't wait till you get a carriage for me.
I've urgent private affairs—in the south—at Marwar."

He shambled out of the office and departed in
the direction of the Deputy Commissioner's
house.   That day at noon I had occasion to go
down the blinding hot Mall, and I saw a crooked
man crawling along the white dust of the roadside, his hat in his hand, quavering dolorously
after the fashion of street-singers at Home.
There was not a soul in sight, and he was out of
all possible earshot of the houses.   And he sang
through his nose, turning his head from right to
left:

> "The Son of Man goes forth to war,
>   A golden crown to gain ;
>   His blood-red banner streams afar—
>   Who follows in his train ? "

I waited to hear no more, but put the poor
wretch into my carriage and drove him off to the
nearest missionary for eventual transfer to the
Asylum.   He repeated the hymn twice while he
was with me whom he did not in the least

recognize, and I left him singing it to the missionary.

Two days later I inquired after his welfare of the Superintendent of the Asylum.

"He was admitted suffering from sunstroke. He died early yesterday morning," said the Superintendent. "Is it true that he was half an hour bareheaded in the sun at midday?"

"Yes," said I, "but do you happen to know if he had anything upon him by any chance when he died?"

"Not to my knowledge," said the Superintendent.

And there the matter rests.

"THE FINEST STORY IN THE WORLD"

"THE FINEST STORY IN THE WORLD"

> " Or ever the knightly years were gone
>   With the old world to the grave,
> I was a king in Babylon
>   And you were a Christian slave."
>   — *W. E. Henley.*

HIS name was Charlie Mears; he was the only son of his mother who was a widow, and he lived in the north of London, coming into the City every day to work in a bank. He was twenty years old and suffered from aspirations. I met him in a public billiard-saloon where the marker called him by his given name, and he called the marker "Bullseyes." Charlie explained, a little nervously, that he had only come to the place to look on, and since looking on at games of skill is not a cheap amusement for the young, I suggested that Charlie should go back to his mother.

That was our first step toward better acquaintance. He would call on me sometimes in the evenings instead of running about London with his fellow-clerks; and before long, speaking of himself as a young man must, he told me of his

aspirations, which were all literary. He desired
to make himself an undying name chiefly through
verse, though he was not above sending stories
of love and death to the drop-a-penny-in-the-
slot journals. It was my fate to sit still while
Charlie read me poems of many hundred lines,
and bulky fragments of plays that would surely
shake the world. My reward was his unreserved
confidence, and the self-revelations and troubles
of a young man are almost as holy as those of a
maiden. Charlie had never fallen in love, but
was anxious to do so on the first opportunity; he
believed in all things good and all things honor-
able, but, at the same time, was curiously careful
to let me see that he knew his way about the
world as befitted a bank clerk on twenty-five
shillings a week. He rhymed " dove " with
" love " and " moon " with " June," and devoutly
believed that they had never so been rhymed before. The long lame gaps in his plays he filled
up with hasty words of apology and description
and swept on, seeing all that he intended to do
so clearly that he esteemed it already done, and
turned to me for applause.

I fancy that his mother did not encourage his
aspirations, and I know that his writing-table at
home was the edge of his washstand. This he
told me almost at the outset of our acquaintance;
when he was ravaging my bookshelves, and a

little before I was implored to speak the truth as to his chances of "writing something really great, you know." Maybe I encouraged him too much, for, one night, he called on me, his eyes flaming with excitement, and said breathlessly:

"Do you mind—can you let me stay here and write all this evening? I won't interrupt you, I won't really. There's no place for me to write in at my mother's."

"What's the trouble?" I said, knowing well what that trouble was.

"I've a notion in my head that would make the most splendid story that was ever written. Do let me write it out here. It's *such* a notion!"

There was no resisting the appeal. I set him a table; he hardly thanked me, but plunged into the work at once. For half an hour the pen scratched without stopping. Then Charlie sighed and tugged his hair. The scratching grew slower, there were more erasures, and at last ceased. The finest story in the world would not come forth.

"It looks such awful rot now," he said, mournfully. "And yet it seemed so good when I was thinking about it. What's wrong?"

I could not dishearten him by saying the truth. So I answered: "Perhaps you don't feel in the mood for writing."

"Yes I do—except when I look at this stuff. Ugh!"

"Read me what you've done," I said.

"He read, and it was wondrous bad, and he paused at all the specially turgid sentences, expecting a little approval; for he was proud of those sentences, as I knew he would be.

"It needs compression," I suggested, cautiously.

"I hate cutting my things down. I don't think you could alter a word here without spoiling the sense. It reads better aloud than when I was writing it."

"Charlie, you're suffering from an alarming disease afflicting a numerous class. Put the thing by, and tackle it again in a week."

"I want to do it at once. What do you think of it?"

"How can I judge from a half-written tale? Tell me the story as it lies in your head."

Charlie told, and in the telling there was everything that his ignorance had so carefully prevented from escaping into the written word. I looked at him, and wondering whether it were possible that he did not know the originality, the power of the notion that had come in his way? It was distinctly a Notion among notions. Men had been puffed up with pride by notions not a tithe as excellent and practicable. But Charlie babbled on serenely, interrupting the current of pure fancy with samples of horrible sentences that he purposed to use. I heard him out to the end. It would be folly to allow his idea to remain in his own inept hands, when I could do so much with it. Not all that could be done indeed; but, oh so much!

"What do you think?" he said, at last. "I fancy I shall call it 'The Story of a Ship.'"

"I think the idea's pretty good; but you won't be able to handle it for ever so long. Now I"—

"Would it be of any use to you? Would you care to take it? I should be proud," said Charlie, promptly.

There are few things sweeter in this world than the guileless, hot-headed, intemperate, open admiration of a junior. Even a woman in her blindest devotion does not fall into the gait of the man she adores, tilt her bonnet to the angle at which he wears his hat, or interlard her speech with his pet oaths. And Charlie did all these things. Still it was necessary to salve my conscience before I possessed myself of Charlie's thoughts.

"Let's make a bargain. I'll give you a fiver for the notion," I said.

Charlie became a bank-clerk at once.

"Oh, that's impossible. Between two pals, you know, if I mav call you so, and speaking as a man of the world, I couldn't. Take the notion if it's any use to you. I've heaps more."

He had—none knew this better than I—but they were the notions of other men.

"Look at it as a matter of business—between men of the world," I returned. "Five pounds will buy you any number of poetry-books. Business is business, and you may be sure I shouldn't give that price unless "—

"Oh, if you put it *that* way," said Charlie, visibly moved by the thought of the books. The bargain was clinched with an agreement that he should at unstated intervals come to me with all the notions that he possessed, should have a table of his own to write at, and unquestioned right to inflict upon me all his poems and fragments of poems. Then I said, "Now tell me how you came by this idea."

"It came by itself." Charlie's eyes opened a little.

"Yes, but you told me a great deal about the hero that you must have read before somewhere."

"I haven't any time for reading, except when you let me sit here, and on Sundays I'm on my bicycle or down the river all day. There's nothing wrong about the hero, is there?"

"Tell me again and I shall understand clearly. You say that your hero went pirating. How did he live?"

"He was on the lower deck of this ship-thing that I was telling you about."

"What sort of ship?"

"It was the kind rowed with oars, and the sea spurts through the oar-holes and the men row sitting up to their knees in water. Then there's a bench running down between the two lines of oars and an overseer with a whip walks up and down the bench to make the men work."

"How do you know that?"

"It's in the tale. There's a rope running overhead, looped to the upper deck, for the overseer to catch hold of when the ship rolls. When the overseer misses the rope once and falls among the rowers, remember the hero laughs at him and gets licked for it. He's chained to his oar of course—the hero."

"How is he chained?"

"With an iron band round his waist fixed to the bench he sits on, and a sort of handcuff on his left wrist chaining him to the oar. He's on the lower deck where the worst men are sent, and the only light comes from the hatchways and through the oar-holes. Can't you imagine the sunlight just squeezing through between the handle and the hole and wobbling about as the ship moves?"

"I can, but I can't imagine your imagining it."

"How could it be any other way? Now you

listen to me. The long oars on the upper deck are managed by four men to each bench, the lower ones by three, and the lowest of all by two. Remember it's quite dark on the lowest deck and all the men there go mad. When a man dies at his oar on that deck he isn't thrown overboard, but cut up in his chains and stuffed through the oar-hole in little pieces."

"Why?" I demanded, amazed, not so much at the information as the tone of command in which it was flung out.

"To save trouble and to frighten the others. It needs two overseers to drag a man's body up to the top deck; and if the men at the lower deck oars were left alone, of course they'd stop rowing and try to pull up the benches by all standing up together in their chains."

"You've a most provident imagination. Where have you been reading about galleys and galley-slaves?"

"Nowhere that I remember. I row a little when I get the chance. But, perhaps, if you say so, I may have read something."

He went away shortly afterward to deal with booksellers, and I wondered how a bank clerk aged twenty could put into my hands with a profligate abundance of detail, all given with absolute assurance, the story of extravagant and bloodthirsty adventure, riot, piracy, and death in unnamed seas. He had led his hero a desperate dance through revolt against the overseers, to command of a ship of his own, and ultimate establishment of a kingdom on an island "somewhere in the sea, you know"; and, delighted with my paltry five pounds, had gone out to buy the notions of other men, that these might teach him how to write. I had the consolation of knowing that this notion was mine by right of purchase, and I thought that I could make something of it.

When next he came to me he was drunk—royally drunk on many poets for the first time revealed to him. His pupils were dilated, his words tumbled over each other, and he wrapped himself in quotations. Most of all was he drunk with Longfellow.

"Isn't it splendid? Isn't it superb?" he cried, after hasty greetings. "Listen to this—

> "'Wouldst thou,'—so the helmsman answered,
> 'Know the secret of the sea?
> Only those who brave its dangers
> Comprehend its mystery.'

By gum!

> "'Only those who brave its dangers
> Comprehend its mystery,'"

he repeated twenty times, walking up and down the room and forgetting me. "But *I* can understand it too," he said to himself. "I don't know how to thank you for that fiver. And this; listen —

> " ' I remember the black wharves and the ships
> And the sea-tides tossing free,
> And the Spanish sailors with bearded lips,
> And the beauty and mystery of the ships,
> And the magic of the sea.'

I haven't braved any dangers, but I feel as if I knew all about it."

"You certainly seem to have a grip of the sea. Have you ever seen it?"

"When I was a little chap I went to Brighton once; we used to live in Coventry, though, before we came to London. I never saw it,

> " ' When descends on the Atlantic
> The gigantic
> Storm-wind of the Equinox.' "

He shook me by the shoulder to make me understand the passion that was shaking himself.

"When that storm comes," he continued, "I think that all the oars in the ship that I was talking about get broken, and the rowers have their chests smashed in by the bucking oar-heads. By the way, have you done anything with that notion of mine yet?"

"No. I was waiting to hear more of it from you. Tell me how in the world you're so certain about the fittings of the ship. You know nothing of ships."

"I don't know. It's as real as anything to me until I try to write it down. I was thinking about it only last night in bed, after you had loaned me 'Treasure Island'; and I made up a whole lot of new things to go into the story."

"What sort of things?"

"About the food the men ate; rotten figs and black beans and wine in a skin bag, passed from bench to bench."

"Was the ship built so long ago as *that*?"

"As what? I don't know whether it was long ago or not. It's only a notion, but sometimes it seems just as real as if it was true. Do I bother you with talking about it?"

"Not in the least. Did you make up anything else?"

"Yes, but it's nonsense." Charlie flushed a little.

"Never mind; let's hear about it."

"Well, I was thinking over the story, and after awhile I got out of bed and wrote down on a piece of paper the sort of stuff the men might be supposed to scratch on their oars with the edges of their handcuffs. It seemed to make the thing more lifelike. It *is* so real to me, y'know."

"Have you the paper on you?"

"Ye-es, but what's the use of showing it? It's only a lot of scratches. All the same, we might have 'em reproduced in the book on the front page."

"I'll attend to those details. Show me what your men wrote."

He pulled out of his pocket a sheet of note-paper, with a single line of scratches upon it, and I put this carefully away.

"What is it supposed to mean in English?" I said.

"Oh, I don't know. Perhaps it means 'I'm beastly tired.' It's great nonsense," he repeated, "but all those men in the ship seem as real as people to me. Do do something to the notion soon; I should like to see it written and printed."

"But all you've told me would make a long book."

"Make it then. You've only to sit down and write it out."

"Give me a little time. Have you any more notions?"

"Not just now. I'm reading all the books I've bought. They're splendid."

When he had left I looked at the sheet of note-paper with the inscription upon it. Then I took my head tenderly between both hands, to make certain that it was not coming off or turning

round. Then . . . but there seemed to be
no interval between quitting my rooms and finding myself arguing with a policeman outside a
door marked *Private* in a corridor of the British
Museum. All I demanded, as politely as possible, was "the Greek antiquity man." The policeman knew nothing except the rules of the
Museum, and it became necessary to forage
through all the houses and offices inside the
gates. An elderly gentleman called away from
his lunch put an end to my search by holding the
note-paper between finger and thumb and sniff-
ing at it scornfully.

"What does this mean? H'mm," said he.
"So far as I can ascertain it is an attempt to
write extremely corrupt Greek on the part"—
here he glared at me with intention—"of an extremely illiterate—ah—person." He read slowly
from the paper, *"Pollock, Erckmann, Tauchnitz,
Henniker"*—four names familiar to me.

"Can you tell me what the corruption is supposed to mean—the gist of the thing?" I asked.

"I have been—many times—overcome with
weariness in this particular employment. That
is the meaning." He returned me the paper, and
I fled without a word of thanks, explanation, or
apology.

I might have been excused for forgetting much.
To me of all men had been given the chance to

write the most marvelous tale in the world,
nothing less than the story of a Greek galley-
slave, as told by himself. Small wonder that his
dreaming had seemed real to Charlie. The Fates
that are so careful to shut the doors of each suc-
cessive life behind us had, in this case, been
neglectful, and Charlie was looking, though that
he did not know, where never man had been
permitted to look with full knowledge since Time
began. Above all, he was absolutely ignorant
of the knowledge sold to me for five pounds;
and he would retain that ignorance, for bank-
clerks do not understand metempsychosis, and a
sound commercial education does not include
Greek. He would supply me—here I capered
among the dumb gods of Egypt and laughed in
their battered faces—with material to make my
tale sure—so sure that the world would hail it as
an impudent and vamped fiction. And I—I
alone would know that it was absolutely and
literally true. I,—I alone held this jewel to my
hand for the cutting and polishing. Therefore I
danced again among the gods till a policeman
saw me and took steps in my direction.

It remained now only to encourage Charlie to
talk, and here there was no difficulty. But I had
forgotten those accursed books of poetry. He
came to me time after time, as useless as a sur-
charged phonograph—drunk on Byron, Shelley, or

Keats. Knowing now what the boy had been in his past lives, and desperately anxious not to lose one word of his babble, I could not hide from him my respect and interest. He misconstrued both into respect for the present soul of Charlie Mears, to whom life was as new as it was to Adam, and interest in his readings; and stretched my patience to breaking point by reciting poetry—not his own now, but that of others. I wished every English poet blotted out of the memory of mankind. I blasphemed the mightiest names of song because they had drawn Charlie from the path of direct narrative, and would, later, spur him to imitate them; but I choked down my impatience until the first flood of enthusiasm should have spent itself and the boy returned to his dreams.

"What's the use of my telling you what *I* think, when these chaps wrote things for the angels to read?" he growled, one evening. "Why don't you write something like theirs?"

"I don't think you're treating me quite fairly," I said, speaking under strong restraint.

"I've given you the story," he said, shortly, replunging into "Lara."

"But I want the details."

"The things I make up about that damned ship that you call a galley? They're quite easy. You can just make 'em up yourself. Turn up the gas a little, I want to go on reading."

I could have broken the gas globe over his head for his amazing stupidity. I could indeed make up things for myself did I only know what Charlie did not know that he knew. But since the doors were shut behind me I could only wait his youthful pleasure and strive to keep him in good temper. One minute's want of guard might spoil a priceless revelation: now and again he would toss his books aside—he kept them in my rooms, for his mother would have been shocked at the waste of good money had she seen them—and launched into his sea dreams. Again I cursed all the poets of England. The plastic mind of the bank-clerk had been overlaid, colored and distorted by that which he had read, and the result as delivered was a confused tangle of other voices most like the muttered song through a City telephone in the busiest part of the day.

He talked of the galley—his own galley had he but known it—with illustrations borrowed from the "Bride of Abydos." He pointed the experiences of his hero with quotations from "The Corsair," and threw in deep and desperate moral reflections from "Cain" and "Manfred," expecting me to use them all. Only when the talk turned on Longfellow were the jarring cross-currents dumb, and I knew that Charlie was speaking the truth as he remembered it.

"What do you think of this?" I said one evening, as soon as I understood the medium in which his memory worked best, and, before he could expostulate, read him the whole of "The Saga of King Olaf!"

He listened open-mouthed, flushed, his hands drumming on the back of the sofa where he lay, till I came to the Song of Einar Tamberskelver and the verse:

> "Einar then, the arrow taking
>   From the loosened string,
>   Answered: 'That was Norway breaking
>   'Neath thy hand, O King.'"

He gasped with pure delight of sound.

"That's better than Byron, a little," I ventured.

"Better? Why it's *true!* How could he have known?"

I went back and repeated:

> "'What was that?' said Olaf, standing
>   On the quarter-deck,
>   'Something heard I like the stranding
>   Of a shattered wreck?'"

"How could he have known how the ships crash and the oars rip out and go *z-zzp* all along the line? Why only the other night. . . . But go back please and read The Skerry of Shrieks' again."

"No, I'm tired. Let's talk. What happened
the other night?"

"I had an awful nightmare about that galley
of ours. I dreamed I was drowned in a fight.
You see we ran alongside another ship in harbor.
The water was dead still except where our oars
whipped it up. You know where I always sit
in the galley?" He spoke haltingly at first, under a fine English fear of being laughed at.

"No. That's news to me," I answered,
meekly, my heart beginning to beat.

"On the fourth oar from the bow on the right
side on the upper deck. There were four of us
at that oar, all chained. I remember watching
the water and trying to get my handcuffs off before the row began. Then we closed up on the
other ship, and all their fighting men jumped over
our bulwarks, and my bench broke and I was
pinned down with the three other fellows on top
of me, and the big oar jammed across our backs."

"Well?" Charlie's eyes were alive and alight.
He was looking at the wall behind my chair.

"I don't know how we fought. The men
were trampling all over my back, and I lay low.
Then our rowers on the left side—tied to their
oars, you know—began to yell and back water.
I could hear the water sizzle, and we spun round
like a cockchafer and I knew, lying where I was,
that there was a galley coming up bow-on, to

ram us on the left side. I could just lift up my
head and see her sail over the bulwarks. We
wanted to meet her bow to bow, but it was too
late. We could only turn a little bit because the
galley on our right had hooked herself on to us
and stopped our moving. Then, by gum! there
was a crash! Our left oars began to break as the
other galley, the moving one y'know, stuck her
nose into them. Then the lower-deck oars shot
up through the deck planking, butt first, and one
of them jumped clean up into the air and came
down again close to my head."

"How was that managed?"

"The moving galley's bow was plunking them
back through their own oar-holes, and I could
hear the devil of a shindy in the decks below.
Then her nose caught us nearly in the middle,
and we tilted sideways, and the fellows in the
right-hand galley unhitched their hooks and
ropes, and threw things on to our upper deck—
arrows, and hot pitch or something that stung,
and we went up and up and up on the left side,
and the right side dipped, and I twisted my head
round and saw the water stand still as it topped
the right bulwarks, and then it curled over and
crashed down on the whole lot of us on the right
side, and I felt it hit my back, and I woke."

"One minute, Charlie. When the sea topped
the bulwarks, what did it look like?" I had my

reasons for asking. A man of my acquaintance had once gone down with a leaking ship in a still sea, and had seen the water-level pause for an instant ere it fell on the deck.

"It looked just like a banjo-string drawn tight, and it seemed to stay there for years," said Charlie.

Exactly! The other man had said: "It looked like a silver wire laid down along the bulwarks, and I thought it was never going to break." He had paid everything except the bare life for this little valueless piece of knowledge, and I had traveled ten thousand weary miles to meet him and take his knowledge at second hand. But Charlie, the bank-clerk on twenty-five shillings a week, he who had never been out of sight of a London omnibus, knew it all. It was no consolation to me that once in his lives he had been forced to die for his gains. I also must have died scores of times, but behind me, because I could have used my knowledge, the doors were shut.

"And then?" I said, trying to put away the devil of envy.

"The funny thing was, though, in all the mess I didn't feel a bit astonished or frightened. It seemed as if I'd been in a good many fights, because I told my next man so when the row began. But that cad of an overseer on my deck wouldn't unloose our chains and give us a chance.

He always said that we'd all be set free after a battle, but we never were; we never were." Charlie shook his head mournfully.

"What a scoundrel!"

"I should say he was. He never gave us enough to eat, and sometimes we were so thirsty that we used to drink salt-water. I can taste that salt-water still."

"Now tell me something about the harbor where the fight was fought."

"I didn't dream about that. I know it was a harbor, though; because we were tied up to a ring on a white wall and all the face of the stone under water was covered with wood to prevent our ram getting chipped when the tide made us rock."

"That's curious. Our hero commanded the galley, didn't he?"

"Didn't he just! He stood by the bows and shouted like a good 'un. He was the man who killed the overseer."

"But you were all drowned together, Charlie, weren't you?"

"I can't make that fit quite," he said, with a puzzled look. "The galley must have gone down with all hands, and yet I fancy that the hero went on living afterward. Perhaps he climbed into the attacking ship. I wouldn't see that, of course. I was dead, you know."

He shivered slightly and protested that he could remember no more.

I did not press him further, but to satisfy myself that he lay in ignorance of the workings of his own mind, deliberately introduced him to Mortimer Collins's "Transmigration," and gave him a sketch of the plot before he opened the pages.

"What rot it all is!" he said, frankly, at the end of an hour. "I don't understand his nonsense about the Red Planet Mars and the King, and the rest of it. Chuck me the Longfellow again."

I handed him the book and wrote out as much as I could remember of his description of the seafight, appealing to him from time to time for confirmation of fact or detail. He would answer without raising his eyes from the book, as assuredly as though all his knowledge lay before him on the printed page. I spoke under the normal key of my voice that the current might not be broken, and I know that he was not aware of what he was saying, for his thoughts were out on the sea with Longfellow.

"Charlie," I asked, "when the rowers on the gallies mutinied how did they kill their overseers?"

"Tore up the benches and brained 'em. That happened when a heavy sea was running. An overseer on the lower deck slipped from the centre plank and fell among the rowers. They choked him to death against the side of the ship with their chained hands quite quietly, and it was too dark for the other overseer to see what had happened. When he asked, he was pulled down too and choked, and the lower deck fought their way up deck by deck, with the pieces of the broken benches banging behind 'em. How they howled!"

"And what happened after that?"

"I don't know. The hero went away—red hair and red beard and all. That was after he had captured our galley, I think."

The sound of my voice irritated him, and he motioned slightly with his left hand as a man does when interruption jars.

"You never told me he was red-headed before, or that he captured your galley," I said, after a discreet interval.

Charlie did not raise his eyes.

"He was as red as a red bear," said he, abstractedly. "He came from the north; they said so in the galley when he looked for rowers—not slaves, but free men. Afterward—years and years afterward—news came from another ship, or else he came back"—

His lips moved in silence. He was rapturously retasting some poem before him.

"Where had he been, then?" I was almost whispering that the sentence might come gentle to whichever section of Charlie's brain was working on my behalf.

"To the Beaches—the Long and Wonderful Beaches!" was the reply, after a minute of silence.

"To Furdurstrandi?" I asked, tingling from head to foot.

"Yes, to Furdurstrandi," he pronounced the word in a new fashion. "And I too saw "— The voice failed.

"Do you know what you have said?" I shouted, incautiously.

He lifted his eyes, fully roused now. "No!" he snapped. "I wish you'd let a chap go on reading. Hark to this:

> "'But Othere, the old sea captain,
>   He neither paused nor stirred
>   Till the king listened, and then
>   Once more took up his pen
>   And wrote down every word.
>
> "'And to the King of the Saxons
>   In witness of the truth,
>   Raising his noble head,
>   He stretched his brown hand and said,
>   " Behold this walrus tooth." '

By Jove, what chaps those must have been, to go sailing all over the shop never knowing where they'd fetch the land! Hah!"

"Charlie," I pleaded, "if you'll only be sensible for a minute or two I'll make our hero in our tale every inch as good as Othere."

"Umph! Longfellow wrote that poem. I don't care about writing things any more. I want to read." He was thoroughly out of tune now, and raging over my own ill-luck, I left him.

Conceive yourself at the door of the world's treasure-house guarded by a child—an idle irresponsible child playing knuckle-bones—on whose favor depends the gift of the key, and you will imagine one half my torment. Till that evening Charlie had spoken nothing that might not lie within the experiences of a Greek galley-slave. But now, or there was no virtue in books, he had talked of some desperate adventure of the Vikings, of Thorfin Karlsefne's sailing to Wineland, which is America, in the ninth or tenth century. The battle in the harbor he had seen; and his own death he had described. But this was a much more startling plunge into the past. Was it possible that he had skipped half a dozen lives and was then dimly remembering some episode of a thousand years later? It was a maddening jumble, and the worst of it was that Charlie Mears in his normal condition was the last person in the world to clear it up. I could only wait and watch, but I went to bed that night full of the wildest imaginings. There was nothing that was not possible if Charlie's detestable memory only held good.

I might rewrite the Saga of Thorfin Karlsefne as it had never been written before, might tell the story of the first discovery of America, myself the discoverer. But I was entirely at Charlie's mercy, and so long as there was a three-and-sixpenny Bohn volume within his reach Charlie would not tell. I dared not curse him openly; I hardly dared jog his memory, for I was dealing with the experiences of a thousand years ago, told through the mouth of a boy of to-day; and a boy of to-day is affected by every change of tone and gust of opinion, so that he lies even when he desires to speak the truth.

I saw no more of him for nearly a week. When next I met him it was in Gracechurch Street with a billbook chained to his waist. Business took him over London Bridge and I accompanied him. He was very full of the importance of that book and magnified it. As we passed over the Thames we paused to look at a steamer unloading great slabs of white and brown marble. A barge drifted under the steamer's stern and a lonely cow in that barge bellowed. Charlie's face changed from the face of the bank-clerk to that of an unknown and—though he would not have believed this—a much shrewder man. He flung out his arm across the parapet of the bridge and laughing very loudly, said:

"When they heard *our* bulls bellow the Skrœlings ran away!"

I waited only for an instant, but the barge and the cow had disappeared under the bows of the steamer before I answered.

"Charlie, what do you suppose are Skrœlings?"

"Never heard of 'em before. They sound like a new kind of seagull. What a chap you are for asking questions!" he replied. "I have to go to the cashier of the Omnibus Company yonder. Will you wait for me and we can lunch somewhere together? I've a notion for a poem."

"No, thanks. I'm off. You're sure you know nothing about Skrœlings?"

"Not unless he's been entered for the Liverpool Handicap." He nodded and disappeared in the crowd.

Now it is written in the Saga of Eric the Red or that of Thorfin Karlsefne, that nine hundred years ago when Karlsefne's galleys came to Leif's booths, which Leif had erected in the unknown land called Markland, which may or may not have been Rhode Island, the Skrœlings—and the Lord He knows who these may or may not have been —came to trade with the Vikings, and ran away because they were frightened at the bellowing of the cattle which Thorfin had brought with him in the ships. But what in the world could a Greek slave know of that affair? I wandered up and down among the streets trying to unravel the mystery, and the more I considered it, the more baffling it grew. One thing only seemed certain, and that certainty took away my breath for the moment. If I came to full knowledge of anything at all, it would not be one life of the soul in Charlie Mears's body, but half a dozen—half a dozen several and separate existences spent on blue water in the morning of the world!

Then I walked round the situation.

Obviously if I used my knowledge I should stand alone and unapproachable until all men were as wise as myself. That would be something, but manlike I was ungrateful. It seemed bitterly unfair that Charlie's memory should fail me when I needed it most. Great Powers above —I looked up at them through the fog smoke— did the Lords of Life and Death know what this meant to me? Nothing less than eternal fame of the best kind, that comes from One, and is shared by one alone. I would be content—remembering Clive, I stood astounded at my own moderation,—with the mere right to tell one story, to work out one little contribution to the light literature of the day. If Charlie were permitted full recollection for one hour—for sixty short minutes

—of existences that had extended over a thousand years—I would forego all profit and honor from all that I should make of his speech. I would take no share in the commotion that would follow throughout the particular corner of the earth that calls itself "the world." The thing should be put forth anonymously. Nay, I would make other men believe that they had written it. They would hire bull-hided self-advertising Englishmen to bellow it abroad. Preachers would found a fresh conduct of life upon it, swearing that it was new and that they had lifted the fear of death from all mankind. Every Orientalist in Europe would patronize it discursively with Sanskrit and Pali texts. Terrible women would invent unclean variants of the men's belief for the elevation of their sisters. Churches and religions would war over it. Between the hailing and re-starting of an omnibus I foresaw the scuffles that would arise among half a dozen denominations all professing "the doctrine of the True Metempsychosis as applied to the world and the New Era"; and saw, too, the respectable English newspapers shying, like frightened kine, over the beautiful simplicity of the tale. The mind leaped forward a hundred—two hundred—a thousand years. I saw with sorrow that men would mutilate and garble the story; that rival creeds would turn it upside down till, at last, the western world which clings to the dread of death more closely than the hope of life, would set it aside as an interesting superstition and stampede after some faith so long forgotten that it seemed altogether new. Upon this I changed the terms of the bargain that I would make with the Lords of Life and Death. Only let me know, let me write, the story with sure knowledge that I wrote the truth, and I would burn the manuscript as a solemn sacrifice. Five minutes after the last line was written I would destroy it all. But I must be allowed to write it with absolute certainty.

There was no answer. The flaming colors of an Aquarium poster caught my eye and I wondered whether it would be wise or prudent to lure Charlie into the hands of the professional mesmerist, and whether, if he were under his power, he would speak of his past lives. If he did, and if people believed him . . . but Charlie would be frightened and flustered, or made conceited by the interviews. In either case he would begin to lie, through fear or vanity. He was safest in my own hands.

"They are very funny fools, your English," said a voice at my elbow, and turning round I recognized a casual acquaintance, a young Bengali law student, called Grish Chunder, whose father had sent him to England to become civilized. The old man was a retired native official, and on an income of five pounds a month contrived to allow his son two hundred pounds a year, and the run of his teeth in a city where he could pretend to be the cadet of a royal house, and tell stories of the brutal Indian bureaucrats who ground the faces of the poor.

Grish Chunder was a young, fat, full-bodied Bengali dressed with scrupulous care in frock coat, tall hat, light trousers and tan gloves. But I had known him in the days when the brutal Indian Government paid for his university education, and he contributed cheap sedition to *Sachi Durpan*, and intrigued with the wives of his schoolmates.

"That is very funny and very foolish," he said, nodding at the poster. "I am going down to the Northbrook Club. Will you come too?"

I walked with him for some time. "You are not well," he said. "What is there in your mind? You do not talk."

"Grish Chunder, you've been too well educated to believe in a God, haven't you?"

"Oah, yes, *here!* But when I go home I must conciliate popular superstition, and make ceremonies of purification, and my women will anoint idols."

"And hang up *tulsi* and feast the *purohit*, and take you back into caste again and make a good *khuttri* of you again, you advanced social Freethinker.   And you'll eat *desi* food, and like it all, from the smell in the courtyard to the mustard oil over you."

"I shall very much like it," said Grish Chunder, unguardedly.   "Once a Hindu—always a Hindu. But I like to know what the English think they know."

"I'll tell you something that one Englishman knows.   It's an old tale to you."

I began to tell the story of Charlie in English, but Grish Chunder put a question in the vernacular, and the history went forward naturally in the tongue best suited for its telling.   After all it could never have been told in English.   Grish Chunder heard me, nodding from time to time, and then came up to my rooms where I finished the tale.

"*Beshak*," he said, philosophically.   "*Lekin darwaza band hai.* (Without doubt, but the door is shut.)   I have heard of this remembering of previous existences among my people.   It is of course an old tale with us, but, to happen to an Englishman—a cow-fed *Malechh*—an outcast. By Jove, that is most peculiar!"

"Outcast yourself, Grish Chunder!   You eat cow-beef every day.   Let's think the thing over. The boy remembers his incarnations."

"Does he know that?" said Grish Chunder, quietly, swinging his legs as he sat on my table. He was speaking in English now.

"He does not know anything. Would I speak to you if he did? Go on!"

"There is no going on at all. If you tell that to your friends they will say you are mad and put it in the papers. Suppose, now, you prosecute for libel."

"Let's leave that out of the question entirely. Is there any chance of his being made to speak?"

"There is a chance. Oah, yess! But *if* he spoke it would mean that all this world would end now—*instanto*—fall down on your head. These things are not allowed, you know. As I said, the door is shut."

"Not a ghost of a chance?"

"How can there be? You are a Christi-án, and it is forbidden to eat, in your books, of the Tree of Life, or else you would never die. How shall you all fear death if you all know what your friend does not know that he knows? I am afraid to be kicked, but I am not afraid to die, because I know what I know. You are not afraid to be kicked, but you are afraid to die. If you were not, by God! you English would be all over the shop in an hour, upsetting the balances of power, and making commotions. It would not be good. But no fear. He will remember a little and a little less, and he will call it dreams. Then he will forget altogether. When I passed my First Arts Examination in Calcutta that was all in the cram-book on Wordsworth. Trailing clouds of glory, you know."

"This seems to be an exception to the rule."

"There are no exceptions to rules. Some are not so hard-looking as others, but they are all the same when you touch. If this friend of yours said so-and-so and so-and-so, indicating that he remembered all his lost lives, or one piece of a lost life, he would not be in the bank another hour. He would be what you called sack because he was mad, and they would send him to an asylum for lunatics. You can see that, my friend."

"Of course I can, but I wasn't thinking of him. His name need never appear in the story."

"Ah! I see. That story will never be written. You can try."

"I am going to."

"For your own credit and for the sake of money, *of* course?"

"No. For the sake of writing the story. On my honor that will be all."

"Even then there is no chance. You cannot play with the Gods. It is a very pretty story now. As they say, Let it go on that—I mean at that. Be quick; he will not last long."

"How do you mean?"

"What I say. He has never, so far, thought about a woman."

"Hasn't he, though!" I remembered some of Charlie's confidences.

"I mean no woman has thought about him. When that comes; *bus—hogya*—all up! I know. There are millions of women here. Housemaids, for instance."

I winced at the thought of my story being ruined by a housemaid. And yet nothing was more probable.

Grish Chunder grinned.

"Yes—also pretty girls—cousins of his house, and perhaps *not* of his house. One kiss that he gives back again and remembers will cure all this nonsense, or else " —

"Or else what? Remember he does not know that he knows."

"I know that. Or else, if nothing happens he will become immersed in the trade and the financial speculations like the rest. It must be so. You can see that it must be so. But the woman will come first, *I* think."

There was a rap at the door, and Charlie charged in impetuously. He had been released from office, and by the look in his eyes I could see that he had come over for a long talk; most probably with poems in his pockets. Charlie's poems were very wearying, but sometimes they led him to talk about the galley.

Grish Chunder looked at him keenly for a minute.

"I beg your pardon," Charlie said, uneasily; "I didn't know you had any one with you."

"I am going," said Grish Chunder.

He drew me into the lobby as he departed.

"That is your man," he said, quickly. "I tell you he will never speak all you wish. That is rot—bosh. But he would be most good to make to see things. Suppose now we pretend that it was only play"—I had never seen Grish Chunder so excited—"and pour the ink-pool into his hand. Eh, what do you think? I tell you that he could see *anything* that a man could see. Let me get the ink and the camphor. He is a seer and he will tell us very many things."

"He may be all you say, but I'm not going to trust him to your gods and devils."

"It will not hurt him. He will only feel a little stupid and dull when he wakes up. You have seen boys look into the ink-pool before."

"That is the reason why I am not going to see it any more. You'd better go, Grish Chunder."

He went, declaring far down the staircase that it was throwing away my only chance of looking into the future.

This left me unmoved, for I was concerned for the past, and no peering of hypnotized boys into mirrors and ink-pools would help me to that. But I recognized Grish Chunder's point of view and sympathized with it.

"What a big black brute that was!" said Charlie, when I returned to him. "Well, look here, I've just done a poem; did it instead of playing dominoes after lunch. May I read it?"

"Let me read it to myself."

"Then you miss the proper expression. Besides, you always make my things sound as if the rhymes were all wrong."

"Read it aloud, then. You're like the rest of 'em."

Charlie mouthed me his poem, and it was not much worse than the average of his verses. He had been reading his books faithfully, but he was not pleased when I told him that I preferred my Longfellow undiluted with Charlie.

Then we began to go through the MS. line by line; Charlie parrying every objection and correction with:

"Yes, that may be better, but you don't catch what I'm driving at."

Charles was, in one way at least, very like one kind of poet.

There was a pencil scrawl at the back of the paper and "What's that?" I said.

"Oh that's not poetry at all. It's some rot I wrote last night before I went to bed and it was too much bother to hunt for rhymes; so I made it a sort of blank verse instead."

Here is Charlie's "blank verse":

"We pulled for you when the wind was against us and the
sails were low.
>   *Will you never let us go?*
We ate bread and onions when you took towns or ran aboard
quickly when you were beaten back by the foe,
The captains walked up and down the deck in fair weather
inging songs, but we were below,
We fainted with our chins on the oars and you did not see
that we were idle for we still swung to and fro.
>   *Will you never let us go?*
The salt made the oar handles like sharkskin; our knees
were cut to the bone with salt cracks; our hair was stuck to
our foreheads; and our lips were cut to our gums and you
whipped us because we could not row.
>   *Will you never let us go?*
But in a little time we shall run out of the portholes as the
water runs along the oarblade, and though you tell the others
to row after us you will never catch us till you catch the oar-
thresh and tie up the winds in the belly of the sail. Aho!
>   *Will you never let us go?*"

"H'm.   What's oar-thresh, Charlie?"

"The water washed up by the oars.   That's
the sort of song they might sing in the galley, y'
know.   Aren't you ever going to finish that story
and give me some of the profits?"

"It depends on yourself.   If you had only told
me more about your hero in the first instance it
might have been finished by now.   You're so
hazy in your notions."

"I only want to give you the general notion of
it—the knocking about from place to place and

the fighting and all that. Can't you fill in the rest yourself? Make the hero save a girl on a pirate-galley and marry her or do something."

"You're a really helpful collaborator. I suppose the hero went through some few adventures before he married."

"Well then, make him a very artful card—a low sort of man—a sort of political man who went about making treaties and breaking them— a black-haired chap who hid behind the mast when the fighting began."

"But you said the other day that he was red-haired."

"I couldn't have. Make him black-haired of course. You've no imagination."

Seeing that I had just discovered the entire principles upon which the half-memory falsely called imagination is based, I felt entitled to laugh, but forbore, for the sake of the tale.

"You're right. *You're* the man with imagination. A black-haired chap in a decked ship," I said.

"No, an open ship—like a big boat."

This was maddening.

"Your ship has been built and designed, closed and decked in; you said so yourself," I protested.

"No, no, not that ship. That was open, or half decked because— By Jove you're right.

You made me think of the hero as a red-haired chap. Of course if he were red, the ship would be an open one with painted sails."

Surely, I thought, he would remember now that he had served in two galleys at least—in a three-decked Greek one under the black-haired "political man," and again in a Viking's open sea-serpent under the man "red as a red bear" who went to Markland. The devil prompted me to speak.

"Why, 'of course,' Charlie?" said I.

"I don't know. Are you making fun of me?"

The current was broken for the time being. I took up a notebook and pretended to make many entries in it.

"It's a pleasure to work with an imaginative chap like yourself," I said, after a pause. "The way that you've brought out the character of the hero is simply wonderful."

"Do you think so?" he answered, with a pleased flush. "I often tell myself that there's more in me than my mo— than people think."

"There's an enormous amount in you."

"Then, won't you let me send an essay on The Ways of Bank Clerks to *Tit-Bits*, and get the guinea prize?"

"That wasn't exactly what I meant, old fellow: perhaps it would be better to wait a little and go ahead with the galley-story."

"Ah, but I sha'n't get the credit of that. *Tit-Bits* would publish my name and address if I win. What are you grinning at? They *would*."

"I know it. Suppose you go for a walk. I want to look through my notes about our story."

Now this reprehensible youth who left me, a little hurt and put back, might for aught he or I knew have been one of the crew of the Argo— had been certainly slave or comrade to Thorfin Karlsefne. Therefore he was deeply interested in guinea competitions. Remembering what Grish Chunder had said I laughed aloud. The Lords of Life and Death would never allow Charlie Mears to speak with full knowledge of his pasts, and I must even piece out what he had told me with my own poor inventions while Charlie wrote of the ways of bank-clerks.

I got together and placed on one file all my notes; and the net result was not cheering. I read them a second time. There was nothing that might not have been compiled at second-hand from other people's books—except, per-haps, the story of the fight in the harbor. The adventures of a Viking had been written many times before; the history of a Greek galley-slave was no new thing, and though I wrote both, who could challenge or confirm the accuracy of my details? I might as well tell a tale of two thousand years hence. The Lords of Life and

Death were as cunning as Grish Chunder had
hinted. They would allow nothing to escape
that might trouble or make easy the minds of
men. Though I was convinced of this, yet I
could not leave the tale alone. Exaltation followed reaction, not once, but twenty times in
the next few weeks. My moods varied with the
March sunlight and flying clouds. By night or
in the beauty of a spring morning I perceived
that I could write that tale and shift continents
thereby. In the wet, windy afternoons, I saw
that the tale might indeed be written, but would
be nothing more than a faked, false-varnished,
sham-rusted piece of Wardour Street work at
the end. Then I blessed Charlie in many ways
—though it was no fault of his. He seemed to
be busy with prize competitions, and I saw less
and less of him as the weeks went by and the
earth cracked and grew ripe to spring, and the
buds swelled in their sheaths. He did not care
to read or talk of what he had read, and there
was a new ring of self-assertion in his voice. I
hardly cared to remind him of the galley when
we met; but Charlie alluded to it on every occasion, always as a story from which money was
to be made.

"I think I deserve twenty-five per cent., don't
I, at least," he said, with beautiful frankness.
"I supplied all the ideas, didn't I?"

This greediness for silver was a new side in his nature. I assumed that it had been developed in the City, where Charlie was picking up the curious nasal drawl of the underbred City man.

"When the thing's done we'll talk about it. I can't make anything of it at present. Red-haired or black-haired hero are equally difficult."

He was sitting by the fire staring at the red coals. "I can't understand what you find so difficult. It's all as clear as mud to me," he replied. A jet of gas puffed out between the bars, took light and whistled softly. "Suppose we take the red-haired hero's adventures first, from the time that he came south to my galley and captured it and sailed to the Beaches."

I knew better now than to interrupt Charlie. I was out of reach of pen and paper, and dared not move to get them lest I should break the current. The gas-jet puffed and whinnied, Charlie's voice dropped almost to a whisper, and he told a tale of the sailing of an open galley to Furdurstrandi, of sunsets on the open sea, seen under the curve of the one sail evening after evening when the galley's beak was notched into the centre of the sinking disc, and "we sailed by that for we had no other guide," quoth Charlie. He spoke of a landing on an island and explorations in its woods, where the crew killed three men whom they found asleep under the pines.

Their ghosts, Charlie said, followed the galley, swimming and choking in the water, and the crew cast lots and threw one of their number overboard as a sacrifice to the strange gods whom they had offended. Then they ate sea-weed when their provisions failed, and their legs swelled, and their leader, the red-haired man, killed two rowers who mutinied, and after a year spent among the woods they set sail for their own country, and a wind that never failed carried them back so safely that they all slept at night. This, and much more Charlie told. Sometimes the voice fell so low that I could not catch the words, though every nerve was on the strain. He spoke of their leader, the red-haired man, as a pagan speaks of his God; for it was he who cheered them and slew them impartially as he thought best for their needs; and it was he who steered them for three days among floating ice, each floe crowded with strange beasts that "tried to sail with us," said Charlie, "and we beat them back with the handles of the oars."

The gas-jet went out, a burned coal gave way, and the fire settled down with a tiny crash to the bottom of the grate. Charlie ceased speaking, and I said no word.

"By Jove!" he said, at last, shaking his head. "I've been staring at the fire till I'm dizzy. What was I going to say?"

"Something about the galley."

"I remember now. It's 25 per cent. of the profits, isn't it?"

"It's anything you like when I've done the tale."

"I wanted to be sure of that. I must go now. I've—I've an appointment." And he left me.

Had my eyes not been held I might have known that that broken muttering over the fire was the swan-song of Charlie Mears. But I thought it the prelude to fuller revelation. At last and at last I should cheat the Lords of Life and Death!

When next Charlie came to me I received him with rapture. He was nervous and embarrassed, but his eyes were very full of light, and his lips a little parted.

"I've done a poem," he said; and then, quickly: "it's the best I've ever done. Read it." He thrust it into my hand and retreated to the window.

I groaned inwardly. It would be the work of half an hour to criticise—that is to say praise— the poem sufficiently to please Charlie. Then I had good reason to groan, for Charlie, discarding his favorite centipede metres, had launched into shorter and choppier verse, and verse with a motive at the back of it. This is what I read:

> " The day is most fair, the cheery wind
>   Halloos behind the hill,
>   Where he bends the wood as seemeth good,
>   And the sapling to his will!
>   Riot O wind; there is that in my blood
>   That would not have thee still!
>
> " She gave me herself, O Earth, O Sky;
>   Grey sea, she is mine alone!
>   Let the sullen boulders hear my cry,
>   And rejoice tho' they be but stone!
>
> " Mine! I have won her O good brown earth,
>   Make merry! 'Tis hard on Spring;
>   Make merry; my love is doubly worth
>   All worship your fields can bring!
>   Let the hind that tills you feel my mirth
>   At the early harrowing."

"Yes, it's the early harrowing, past a doubt," I said, with a dread at my heart. Charlie smiled, but did not answer.

> " Red cloud of the sunset, tell it abroad;
>   I am victor. Greet me O Sun,
>   Dominant master and absolute lord
>   Over the soul of one!"

" Well?" said Charlie, looking over my shoulder.

I thought it far from well, and very evil indeed, when he silently laid a photograph on the paper —the photograph of a girl with a curly head, and a foolish slack mouth.

"Isn't it—isn't it wonderful?" he whispered, pink to the tips of his ears, wrapped in the rosy mystery of first love. "I didn't know; I didn't think—it came like a thunderclap."

"Yes. It comes like a thunderclap. Are you very happy, Charlie?"

"My God—she—she loves me!" He sat down repeating the last words to himself. I looked at the hairless face, the narrow shoulders already bowed by desk-work, and wondered when, where, and how he had loved in his past lives.

"What will your mother say?" I asked, cheerfully.

"I don't care a damn what she says."

At twenty the things for which one does not care a damn should, properly, be many, but one must not include mothers in the list. I told him this gently; and he described Her, even as Adam must have described to the newly named beasts the glory and tenderness and beauty of Eve. Incidentally I learned that She was a tobacconist's assistant with a weakness for pretty dress, and had told him four or five times already that She had never been kissed by a man before.

Charlie spoke on and on, and on; while I, separated from him by thousands of years, was considering the beginnings of things. Now I understood why the Lords of Life and Death shut the doors so carefully behind us. It is that we may not remember our first wooings. Were it not so, our world would be without inhabitants in a hundred years.

"Now, about that galley-story," I said, still more cheerfully, in a pause in the rush of the speech.

Charlie looked up as though he had been hit. "The galley—what galley? Good heavens, don't joke, man! This is serious! You don't know how serious it is!"

Grish Chunder was right. Charlie had tasted the love of woman that kills remembrance, and the finest story in the world would never be written.